D0916049

LOST FAITH

A Practical Theology for Post-Christendom Ministry

Seth Bouchelle

JOHNSON
UNIVERSITY
FLORIDA
LIBRARY

Urban Loft Publishers | Skyforest, CA

Lost Faith
A Practical Theology for Post-Christendom Ministry

Copyright © 2020 Seth Bouchelle

All rights reserved. Except for brief quotations in critical publications or reviews, no part of this book may be reproduced in any manner without prior written permission from the publisher. Write: Permissions, Urban Loft Publishers, P.O. Box 6
Skyforest, CA, 92385.

Urban Loft Publishers
P.O. Box 6
Skyforest, CA 92385
www.urbanloftpublishers.com

Senior Editors: Stephen Burris & Kendi Howells Douglas
Copy Editor: Christian Arnold & Marla Black
Track Editor: Jared Looney
Graphics: Brittnay Parsons
Cover Design: Elisabeth Arnold

Scripture quotations are taken from the *Holy Bible*, New Living Translation, copyright © 1996, 2004, 2015 by Tyndale House Foundation. Used by permission of Tyndale House Publishers, Inc., Carol Stream, Illinois 60188. All rights reserved.

ISBN-13: 978-1-949-625-51-6

Made in the U.S

Praise for *Lost Faith*

"Missiology has desperately needed a fresh voice with practical examples of a lived theology. <u>Lost Faith</u> weaves together the delicate nuances of complex urban relationships with sound biblical theology. This work will serve as an essential field guide for our leaders."

　　　-Joe Reed, Founder and President of *Exponent Group*

"It has been said that the overarching concern for people living in Western culture today is the search for meaning and purpose. Through personal experience, Seth Bouchelle weaves together a thick description of the lives of people he encounters everyday who are searching for something - a home, for identity, for relationship, for love. They are "Lost." Bouchelle does not mean this pejoratively, but as a description of our common cultural experience as seekers of something. We are all on a journey, not always sure exactly where we are going or how we might get there – in this sense "Lost." But because we are actively seeking, we have inherently assumed the posture of a disciple. "Lost Faith" is book on ministry and evangelism in a Post-Christendom context that is theologically formed and sociologically informed. Using the diverse tapestry of biblical and theological language and imagery, Bouchelle offers a paradigm for evangelism/ministry that engages the complexities of a diverse Postmodern and Post-Christian culture. Bouchelle does not take for granted his own faith in his interactions with those that don't share his faith. Instead, he encourages people of faith to go on a journey with others to discover through diverse Christian community, imagery and language the meaning and purpose that we seek. This book will not only be a great resource for the practice of ministry and evangelism, but will help us imagine what faith looks like in a Postmodern and Post-Christian world."

- Ben Langford, Director of the Center for Global Missions at Oklahoma Christian

In the world of mission, "Disciple-Making Movements", "Disciples making disciples", and new paradigms of church are the new trendy terms. As Seth mentions, the church and its North American context look very different from a decade or two ago and will look indiscernible in another decade. It takes a new mindset to effectively and faithfully make disciples and plant healthy churches in this changing context. In the urban, Western context, I know of no one who is seeing the fruitfulness that Seth is seeing in NYC. I have found his work a gift in my own understanding of discipleship and training others in mission. I unreservedly recommend Lost Faith to two groups of people: 1) Those who are training in mission, this resource will open a new world of thought and practice while challenging traditional approaches to learning and training. 2) Those like me who find themselves in the midst of a paradigm shift from traditional church to a focus on new forms of disciple-making, this will serve as an encouraging example of a movement in its infancy which promises significant growth and multiplication. Be prepared to be challenged and stretched while being given new eyes to see.

-David Fittro, Director, EQUIP Britain

Table of Contents

Introduction

Imagine that you are touring a location, like a school campus. This is a place not completely unfamiliar to you, but, as you look around the grounds, you find that the layout is not completely navigable either. There are new buildings, the current landscaping is different than you remember it, you do not recognize the names of the administrators, some of the facilities have been repurposed since you last visited. All of this leaves you feeling disoriented and a bit uncertain of how to proceed to where you wish to go. This experience - an analogy I frequently use at the beginning of my work as a spiritual director - might also apply well to the task of doing theology for contemporary urban and post-Christendom ministry.

As both an active church planter in New York City and a millennial I frequently find myself expected to speak on behalf of the emerging urban Post-Christendom[1] culture in the United States. I am treated, at times, as if my age and vocation qualify me as "an expert" on this topic. In truth, I must admit that I am no such thing. However, I would like, in these pages, to offer a few thoughts and stories from my work as an evangelist and church planter among the Lost of urban America. It is my hope that this may contribute in some small way to sharpening the ministerial tools of others who are seeking

---

[1] Stuart Murray defines Post-Christendom as "the culture that emerges as the Christian faith loses coherence within a society that has been definitively shaped by the Christian story and as the institutions that have been developed to express Christian convictions decline in influence." Murray, *Post-Christendom: Church and Ministry in a Strange New World* (Paternoster Press: Colorado Springs, CO, 2004), 15.

to work for the Kingdom of God in the continually emerging urban and Post-Christendom culture of North America.[2]

At the time of this writing I minister to several dozen individuals, almost none of whom identified as "Christian" when they first joined our communities. Many of them have been part of our communities for some time and still are not baptized followers of Jesus. These are my friends and my church. I know them, and I love them. I know their fears, their hopes, their failures, and their questions. Many of these I share. I have been present for some of the most transformative spiritual breakthroughs in their lives, and I have walked through the frustratingly slow dying-off of spiritual immaturity which accompanies all ministry, but especially ministry among those outside of the established church. The Lost share their lives and their world with me, as I share mine with them. This is the perspective from which I write.

In this work I would like to walk you through an orientation of the world where people like my friends, the Lost, live. I recognize that this is territory (both theologically and ethnographically) which is not completely foreign to most readers. I am not, therefore, interested in sharing a groundbreaking ministry strategy or new systematic theology. Nor am I writing a critique of traditional or contemporary theological frameworks. I will assume that you already know most of "the campus" of our culture, which is why this book is simply a reorientation for those who may have not toured the grounds in a while.

There has been some remodeling in recent years, and I have spent a great deal of time in some of the new additions. Many people - including those who have left, who struggle with, or who do not identify with traditional Christian institutions - are asking questions and interpreting the gospel through sets of experiences that may be unfamiliar to those who have spent their life in congregational ministry. If these changes make you feel

---

[2] For more on urbanization and globalization in North America, see Jared Looney, *Crossroads of the Nations* (Urban Loft Publishers: Portland, OR, 2015), 35-60.

disoriented, I would be happy to show you around to the best of my abilities. This book is my attempt to do just that.

There are two primary audiences I have tried to consider as I composed this book. The first is my fellow vocational ministers. We workers - both in the mission field and the professional church world - are often guilty of looking for the latest technique, the newest strategy, and the most cutting edge tools, but we frequently view the difficult work of theology as, at best, elitist and unnecessary, and, at worst, dangerous and anti-ministry. Even among my more studiously inclined ministry peers I find that the strain of rethinking theology which accompanies most people's seminary experience and acculturation in the early years of ministry often renders us less inclined to call back into question those things which we, with genuine dissonance, have already had to sort through and decide. For readers with a similar disposition I ask that you take this book as a reorientation. The world of North American urban ministry is not the same as it was 20 or even 10 years ago. I suspect it will not be the same 20 years from now. It is time that we revisit some of the questions and many of the answers which have guided our work.

The other audience I have worked to consider is those working among the professional class of academic theologians. I have found, in my work within the religious academy, that an apparent divide frequently exists between the "pressing questions" of the student of theology and the questions my friends among the Lost find most pressing. This is not a condemnation of the halls of scholarship, nor a calling to account of the seminary. Rather, it is simply a request that those readers who are among my more scholarly sisters and brothers allow the thoughts contained here to challenge, however briefly, some of the assumptions about how our current theologies fit into the emerging cultural contexts of urban Post-Christendom.

Before continuing, I would like to say a quick word on terminology. I struggle to know what to call my friends in ministry. Most of the language that comes readily to mind is either inaccurate or strikes me a pejorative. They are not "unbelievers," not all are "non-Christians," some but not all are "unchurched," only a few are truly "religiously unaffiliated" (what is increasingly becoming known as "the nones") although most would probably check that box on a census. The most respectful language I could find for the present is the traditional designation, the Lost - if for no other reason than because our traditional Christian institutions have lost their interest and lost their being counted among our ranks. But, also, because these individuals find themselves at a loss when trying to articulate their religious identity: in a world full of available religious allegiances, theirs have been lost. As I hope you shall see, (and to any of my Lost friends reading this), I mean this designation with the utmost respect and in that vein, I think it is high time we redefine it.

In summary, I am here to help be a guide. On this new post-Christendom campus, I do not teach any of the classes, and I don't have any authority with the Head Office, but I do know my way around the grounds. I would be happy to help direct you where you want to go, to try and help you select the right teachers for what you want to learn, and, if you get lost, I generally know how to help you get back to where you were trying to get to. It is my hope that, by the end of this work, you are better oriented and equipped to navigate life and ministry among the Lost in our post-Christendom Urban context, and that the thoughts and reflections contained here are a blessing to you and to God's church. Let's begin our tour...

Section I

Laying the Foundation

Chapter 1

Who and What Are We Talking About? An Ethnography of "Lostness"

My Friend Juan

My friend Juan moved to the Bronx from Puerto Rico when he was four years old with his mother and two older sisters.[3] In the coming years Juan's mother was to ascend to the status of a highly respected leader in the neighborhood drug trade. Juan and his (by then) seven siblings all dropped out of school in their early teenage years and cyclically transitioned between dealing drugs and various under-the-table jobs throughout the South Bronx. I met Juan at a neighborhood bar where we still meet up a couple of evenings most weeks. Although he has been out of the drug game for over a decade and has held down steady work as a mechanic for the last eighteen years, Juan's life is still very much defined by his years as a gangbanger. He desires it to be this way. One of the only heated moments which has ever taken place between us was when I asked a question about when Juan "used to be" a gangbanger. "What do you mean, 'used to be'? I may not be selling dope anymore, but I didn't 'used to be' nothing," Juan replied proudly, while very obviously readjusting what I took to be a gun under his shirt.

---

[3] Out of respect for privacy, all names used through this work have been changed.

Juan's friends and extended family come from similar backgrounds; most of them have not stepped away from the lifestyle in which they grew up to the extent that Juan has. In his more candid moments, Juan tells me about the fear which accompanied life before he went straight: always looking over his shoulder, worried that the cops were going to catch him or that a rival gang was going to jump him, always afraid to fail his own neighborhood, thus bringing shame on his family. Juan got out of the game after his first child was born. He makes a lot less money now, he tells me, and puts up with a lot more crap from people he doesn't respect, but he never has to wonder when it's going to fall apart.

I first bonded with Juan at our local bar. He subsequently invited me to start going out with his friends and during these outings we would often have deeply spiritual conversations. Many of Juan's coworkers and clients are ex-Catholics; most of them have not set foot in a church since they were children. Juan himself grew up immersed in the world of Santeria.[4] His mother was an initiate and his family never lacks for stories of demonic attack and their mother's counter attacks (you always try to turn a curse back on the one who cursed you, or, as Juan says, "You need stuff that's stronger than their stuff so it bounces back"). I learned many stories of the rites and practices of this popular Spanish folk-religion while preparing to speak at his mother's memorial service, the only occasion when all of the siblings have gotten together in the last five years, despite living within a few miles of each other.

One of Juan's favorite activities is to invite me to disreputable places and introduce me as "his pastor." Once the drugs are hastily put away and people finish recollecting whether or not they've said anything profane enough to feel that they should apologize to me, Juan inevitably says the same thing: "No, no, he's not like that. See the way we're talking like this

---

[4] Santeria is a Caribbean spiritualist religion which emerged from the practices of Yoruba slaves brought to Cuba in the 17th and 18th centuries. For more see Miguel A. De La Torre, *Santeria: The Beliefs and Rituals of a Growing Religion in America* (Eerdmans Publishing: Grand Rapids, MI, 2004), 1-30.

about God and stuff, to him this is church." The reaction from both Juan's family and coworkers to discovering that I am professionally religious has been the same: "You're a pastor?" they ask, "Then why are you here with us?" I have my own, more tactful, answer to this question, in which I explain that I want to be with the people that I think Jesus would spend time with if he were here. This has yet to be taken as anything but a very honoring explanation. My favorite response, however, is Juan's. On one occasion he said, "He's always telling me how Jesus hung out with prostitutes and thieves, so I figured he would like you guys."

A few years into my relationship with Juan, a ministry coworker of mine dropped by the bar where we hang out. I introduced them before slipping away to answer a phone call. While I was gone, my co-worker later informed me, Juan said to him something which I had been trying to assess for some time. He told him, "I have never been religious in my life, religion is not for people like me. But when Seth and I talk about Jesus, I think maybe I believe this stuff." I have had very few friends in my life who are as loyal and as generous as Juan. Blessed are the poor in spirit like Juan and his friends, for theirs is the Kingdom of God.

My Friend KJ

KJ moved to the East Village in Manhattan from LA about six months before I met her. She's a talented musician in her late twenties and we met one night after I saw her perform at a local venue. Originally from New Zealand, KJ's accent is fairly obvious so I tried to initiate some conversation around the fact that I had worked briefly in Australia about five years before. "What kind of work were you doing there?" she asked politely. I told her that I had worked with a few churches in Queensland and, when she asked whether I was a minister, I playfully answered that I'm actually a monk. As KJ now knows, this answer was half true.

Since 2009 I have lived as a lay person under an adjusted Benedictine rule of life. This lifestyle emerged from a neo-monastic community I was a part of in West Texas from 2009-2013. The disciplines of monasticism - particularly solitude, simplicity, and contemplative prayer - are an integral part of my life and my ministry. And, while it is true that my daily life is still structured around the rhythm and practices of this rule of life, the honest fact is that, on this particular night, I felt that if I said that I was a minister, it might have shut the conversation down. It is rare, however, that people are not interested in having further conversation with a monk.

As it turns out, my instincts were on point, and I learned that KJ's life had been heavily influenced by reading the works of such writers as Henri Nouwen and Thomas Merton. In fact, she had just months before been to visit Merton's hermitage at Gethsemani in Kentucky. While she grew up with no religious background whatsoever, KJ developed an interest in Jesus during her teenage years and began to read the gospels on her own initiative. She has not only a surprising knowledge of the spiritual tradition but also a very well-established practice of contemplative prayer. These spiritual practices have helped her grow through the emotional difficulties of immigration, terminated romantic relationships, and the chaotic (and often neurotic) lifestyle of being a professional performer.

However, KJ has never been attracted to church for any extended period of time. She has tried during several different seasons in her life to attend one but says that something in her experiences there often seemed to be missing. She discussed with me the divorce she feels between her church experience and the intentions she sees in Jesus' ministry, and she felt especially under scrutiny by others (both religious and non-) for the role that spirituality played both in her art and personal life. Since moving to New York, she had felt disconnected from community but knew of no good way to pursue her interest in growing spiritually in relationship with others. She identified her chance meeting with me as something perhaps orchestrated by God, as in the days that followed she discovered that she had a small group of friends in the city who shared many of these same feelings and she was able to share with them the fruit of our conversation. These conversations transitioned into a gathering of seekers which evolved over time into a house-church and then into several house-church groups. Blessed are people, like KJ, who are hungry and thirsty to encounter God, for they will be filled.

My Friend Alan

Alan has been part of a few different church groups I have formed in the last few years. Several of these communities were highly dysfunctional, developed serious leadership problems, and dissolved. When I reflect on these experiences, which by any fair definition we might label as ministry failures, it is surprising and humbling that Alan has stuck around. I would like to claim that it is purely an attraction to Jesus which draws him back to our community, but I know a large part of what has kept Alan in my life is the deep friendship between us. Alan, like many who are a part of our church communities, has never claimed the label Christian. I think he is rather skeptical of a number of things he reads in Scripture, and I think he is more skeptical still of a number of those he has met who claim to be Christian. However, Alan is anything but a cynic.

At the time that I met Alan he was completing a PhD program in botany and, as part of his academic fellowship, teaching at a local college. His specialization was in the study of hops and their native uses around the world, and for this reason Alan and I quickly became brewing partners. It has been a good pairing for a hobby: he did not know how to make beer, and I did not have access to a free supply of exotic hops. It would be easy to assume that someone with no formal religious background and Alan's level of scientific training would be "too educated" to consider faith. Such characterizations seem to have held over in our culture from the height of liberalism in the previous few centuries. In my work, however, I have found few people who are as genuinely open and as unashamedly curious about spiritual things as Alan.

Originally from Turkey, Alan's family moved to the US when he was a young child. They moved back to Turkey briefly during some of his childhood years, and then back again to the US for the bulk of his adolescence. Both of his parents are highly educated and have achieved impressive status in their respective fields. Alan's father grew up in a Muslim family, but he and his brother (Alan's Uncle) left faith before establishing families of their own; Alan, then, was raised in a post-Islamic household with little religious instruction of any sort. When he and I met, his most intimate spiritual encounters had taken place through his study of martial arts and his participation in a cohort of Zen practitioners. He quickly became interested in my practice of prayer and we began an informal relationship of spiritual direction around his otherwise normal participation in our church community.

After he had been a member of our community for a couple of months, Alan took me aside one day with a serious question. "I've been reading through the gospels." he said, "I started with Matthew and I'm almost finished with Luke, but I've been meaning to ask you: what's up with Jesus killing that fig tree? If it wasn't the right time for figs, it's seems pretty messed up that he would kill it. If he can do miracles, why didn't he just make it grow figs?" I was surprised to learn that Alan had taken the initiative of reading scripture so quickly on his own, and needless to say I was not expecting to have to do exegesis over coffee this particular day. I share this story to demonstrate the eagerness with which Alan embraced studying the gospels, but it is also worth mentioning that this was never in exchange for his study of Buddhism, or New Age philosophy, or botany. Many of our most fruitful discussions emerge from the intersection of practices, teachings, and beliefs of the various worlds of Alan's searching. Blessed are people like Alan who search for truth with pure hearts, for they will see God.

My Friends Rebekah and Mary

Rebekah was brought to one of our church groups by another leader who I had discipled earlier in my time in New York. I was introduced to her and her "sister" Mary, who was about fifteen years older than her. Mary and Rebekah both grew up around the Washington Heights neighborhood of Manhattan and in the Bronx. Their family is originally from the Dominican Republic. Mary told me about how strict her mother had been, as a member of the Jehovah's Witnesses, and how it had driven all the kids away from religion by the time they were teenagers. Rebekah's religious outlook was fairly neutral at the time that I met her, but Mary continued to carry a lot of guilt and anger from her own upbringing. They continued to come faithfully to the community for a while and, within about six months, they had branched out and started two new church groups out of their home, one of which I went along with to help them establish.

In time, I learned that Mary and Rebekah were actually not sisters. Mary was Rebekah's mother, but, because she had been only fifteen when she gave birth, many people who met them now just assumed that they were siblings and the two just never bothered to correct them. Mary and Rebekah were very faithful to the ministry of the new churches they had started and to their own continued discipleship. However, the first two years of that work were almost unbearably hard. Within a few months after becoming Christians five of their close friends and family died suddenly, then their house was infested with bedbugs, then a sinister spiritual presence began to traumatize Mary in her dreams and during her prayers, and Rebekah's husband filed for divorce and became very hostile towards her and her young daughter, then Mary's ex-boyfriend (the father of her youngest daughter) began coming to the church and this brought out many unresolved hurts.

They felt they were being attacked for making this faith decision. "Our lives fell apart after we decided to become Christians. Nothing bad happened to us for years, but now look. Why would God let this happen?

What did we do to make him angry that he would punish us like this?" These comments and questions became a regular part of our church gatherings. Through this time, I was very thankful for how frequently Jesus and the epistle writers talked about hardship and persecution, because I had very little to say that was of any worth.

Near the end of this period I had a tragedy in my own life. My wife left her faith and decided that she was no longer called to be faithful to our marital vows, as these were taken on the basis of our identity as Christians and our common belief in marriage as something that is from God. With very little warning or explanation she left and I spent the next three years trying to ascertain where she had moved to and trying to procure a divorce. Needless to say I was devastated and it was to my church that I turned for comfort and for care. "I know it's hard," Rebekah texted me late one afternoon, "but it does get better." I believed her, because I had walked with her through the same thing in her own life. Mary checked up on me every few days for the months following and continued to send me scriptures and encouraging notes. Mary's ex-boyfriend, who had not even been baptized yet, made sure to text me, "God is still faithful and He has a plan for you." Blessed are those like Mary and Rebekah who are persecuted because of righteousness, for theirs is the Kingdom of God. And blessed are those, like all of our churches, who mourn, because they will be comforted.

The Lost's Common Heart

We will continue to revisit the stories of these, and others, of my friends going forward, but I wanted to first pause and draw out a few observations which I think may be helpful in defining who the Lost are in the urban North American context. Like my friends discussed here, many people are lost in the sense that they are searching for something. They are searching for a home, for identity, for relationship, for love. They may have a feeling of emptiness and they do not know what to look for to fill it. Whatever it is Lost people are seeking, they have not discovered a way to find it. This searching quality is what makes them Lost, but it is also what qualifies them for discipleship.

Seeking tends to make people good soil. When we go to preach to the Lost, we go looking for those who are searching and receptive. Rather than entering as the bearers of answers to all of life's definitive questions, we often find these individuals when we, too, are asking questions. We identify one another when we, too, are seen as spiritual seekers. The Lost tend to be distrustful of those who cavalierly announce, "I can give you what you're seeking." And are even more turned off by those who might say, "Let me tell you what you're looking for." But I find that nothing attracts Lost people like saying, "I'm seeking a similar thing. Why don't you come follow along and maybe we'll find it together." This is what, in our team's work in NYC, we talk about as **discovery**.

Discovery is an important component of building relationships and of discipling the Lost. However, if we are going to bond with others on the basis of a shared seeking and questioning, it is important that we understand and affirm that this is not a gambit or a technique. We are not deceiving or tricking people, and this is not a strategy for luring the Lost into conversion. What we are doing is cultivating within ourselves the humility and the love of truth which will form us as followers of Jesus into lifelong learners and questioners. We, without denying the aspects of God which we believe to be true and have committed ourselves to, are admitting the continuing degree of our own limitedness and ignorance. We are sharing some of our perpetual Lostness with our neighbor so that they might see how grace-initiated it is "to be found."

We should not be surprised, then, to find that discovery is also a critical part of the way Jesus discipled others. Discovery and seeking are integral to Jesus' formation of followers and are a never-ending part of how leaders in his church are developed. Telling parables to see who was listening, answering difficult questions with counter questions, and sending out workers to help in the harvest long before they ever claimed him as the

Christ and longer still before they recognized that title included a cross: this is a beautiful picture of ministry defined by discovery. It is the way that Jesus chose to go about his mission, and it is an important quality to cultivate in trying to form relationships among the Lost.

Another important aspect to note about my friends is their relationship with traditional religion. The best term I know to use for this is **"acquaintanceship."** My friends know Christianity, but they usually know it the way you know someone you have often heard talked about at a party but have not spent time with yourself. Or maybe the way you know someone who you once went on a date with, but the evening was unpleasant, so you never went out with them again. They are acquainted with Christianity. This level of familiarity produces two seemingly contradictory feelings in most people, what I would call the **curiosity from ignorance** and the **rejection from "knowing."**

For most of my friends, they are genuinely ignorant about the teachings of the Bible and the historical church, the same way that I am almost always ignorant about things from their backgrounds and cultures. Sometimes we use ignorance as a word to demean people or to be dismissive, but ignorance is actually a quality we should try to embrace in the discipleship process and to freely acknowledge in ourselves. I love learning and asking questions. I also love when other people don't know things and need to ask questions. I love it more when they are not ashamed that they don't know things and *want* to ask questions. I love questioners so much that I try to keep them as unsatisfied as I can when they begin coming to our communities.

As often as is possible, I try to not answer the majority of questions when we begin studying the Bible with people. My general practice in Bible studies is to allow a culture of discovery to form based around shared curiosity which stems from common ignorance. When people begin to ask questions I almost always either direct the question to another person in the group - "Did you see anything in the story that answered that?" - or I take them to another scripture that I think engages their question - "What you said reminded me of this other scripture, let's look and see if that answers your question" - or I just genuinely refuse to answer - "That's a really interesting question, would you be sure to bring that up every week until the group feels like they have an answer?"

The reason I can do this without generally frustrating people is because, first, it respects their capacity as thoughtful people to discover; secondly, it is because it does not stifle the very special curiosity that comes with ignorance. When we embrace and develop this curiosity in the discipleship process, one of the great benefits is that we model a means of discipling others that can be reproduced by the Lost as they grow in faith. I ask people very early in their joining our community to begin sharing with their friends and family the things they are discovering. Normally, this would be very difficult. People might say, "But I don't know enough yet" or "Nobody has taught me how." But because new disciples feel affirmed in asking questions and admitting ignorance, their not knowing something is never an obstacle to them sharing the small bit of good news they might have to offer another person. If they are asked something about faith which they do not know, they are generally not threatened by that feeling because we have affirmed the curiosity which comes with ignorance as something important and normal to the discipleship process.

The other part of acquaintanceship is the rejection that comes from "knowing." By this I mean the kind of preconceptions and pre-judgements about faith which comes from being raised in proximity to a culture influenced by historical Christianity. It is nearly impossible to be raised near an important institution and not have some opinion about it; and the church, no matter how "noninstitutional" its expression is, by its nature, an important institution. The Lost are full of opinions about religion, some of which are uninformed, some of which are amusing, and many of which are either painfully correct or not far off. These beliefs and opinions come from the wider media as well as from first-hand experience of religious people and they are often (seemingly) validated by the anecdotal experiences of neighbors and friends.

Those "known" things that lead to rejection may include issues as diverse as the inerrancy of scripture, beliefs about gender and sexuality in the church, the pursuit of or misuse of finances by religious leaders, the role of religion in American government, the sexual scandals and abuses of clergy, the historical authenticity of Jesus, or the enduring racism of the American church. In my work, I have done little good when attempting to argue about many of these things which have fallen into the rejection that comes from the "knowing" of the Lost. This is not to say that these things are not important, or that they should not be addressed, or that I would not like to have a hand in influencing opinions on these matters in the spiritual formation of my friends. My point is that debate and argumentation have not proven the most effective means of accomplishing this. In my experience, it does much more good to be confessional on issues where I believe they are right and to allow most of the other issues to be addressed with more appropriate timing as they gain greater context, or become less distressing or less hurtful to my friends over time.

This brings me to another commonality I would like to draw out from my friends' stories: a **process orientation**. This best describes our team's philosophy of discipleship: that transformation is a process rather than a single event. I do not think there is any question that, in the gospel accounts, discipleship is a process of coming to know who Jesus is. For the twelve, for the 72, for the New Testament church, and for all of us who have dared to attempt to follow the one we call Christ, we begin a journey of following along, observing, trying to obey, and along the way Jesus continues to ask us: "Who do you say I am?" It is a comfort to me that the great confession ends with the "great confessor" rejecting the cross (Mark 8:32), and also that moments before the ascension of Christ the disciples were still asking, "Is it now time for you to restore the Kingdom of Israel?" (Acts 1:6). I have taken more than a little solace in the degree of dysfunction evident in the churches planted by Paul. Whenever our churches break into fights, I generally comfort them in the process of reconciliation by saying, "Well, you guys are still doing better than the church in Corinth." The fruits of my faith and work do not necessarily reach the bar of the apostles, much less of Jesus, but it is comforting that the bar is often not set too terribly high.

The fact is that we, as people, are slow learners and prone to failure. Thankfully we have a merciful God who understood these qualities about us and allows us a long timeline on which to be wrong as we slowly and painfully overcome our ignorance and our preconceptions and discover who Jesus is. I hope that you noticed this quality in the stories of my friends, and I hope that you were not offended by it, if, for no other reason, than because it is my experience of faith as well. I have church plants that were started and led by people who have yet made a decision about their Christian identity. In various seasons I am surrounded by Nicodemuses who cannot seem to make up their mind about who Jesus is but will not leave his orbit either. Some of the great failures and church divisions which have happened in my work have come from those who were quickest to "convert" and slowest to question their own convictions. Some of the most beautiful Kingdom transformations have occurred through the work of individuals who had an embarrassing amount of habitual sin still in their lives (and I suppose that includes myself).[5] While it is not the ideal I pictured when entering into ministry, this does seem to me to be very much in keeping with the process I see in scripture. My hope is that everyone in the faith communities we've started continues to grow into the full stature of Christ, but I think it respects the way God has made us to allow the time to mature, the space to fail, and the grace to be wrong as we attempt to follow Jesus.

The final two commonalities I wish to point out at this time are the **global identity** and the **loss of family** which characterize so many in the

---

[5] The definition of sin and/or Sin in our theology is a complex and important one and will be taken up later in this work.

urban post-Christendom culture of North America. The Lost are an increasingly diverse group of people. In addition to diversity in ethnicity, language, and socio-economic background, they each have so many other heterogeneous elements and experiences which make up their identity. For this reason, it can be difficult to group or to classify them, but we may attempt to do so occasionally for the purpose of trying to understand. This is not so dangerous if we recognize how limited and how artificial these classifications and categories are. These two qualities, however, the global identity and the loss of family, are increasingly becoming a commonality among the Lost. It was not with any intentionality that of my five friends I chose to introduce, none of them is exclusively from the US or grew up in a predominantly Anglo community. Nor was it on purpose that I chose individuals who are closer to their friends and co-workers than to their nuclear families. In fact, thinking about it now, I don't think I have five friends in all of our work who don't fit these two categories!

The urban American mission-field is becoming increasingly populated by global citizens, what our team often calls our "diaspora neighbors."[6] And urban society is also shifting towards a norm I like to refer to as "the framily principle." This is a situation in which individuals have constructed new household units based on affinity groups and other relational networks besides nuclear family ties. If you don't believe me, here is a fun challenge: go look up the two or three most critically praised sitcoms on TV and review the cast of characters. I would be willing to bet that you find they are not stories about a family, in the classical sense, and that they are not all white middle Americans. This shift in the context of the "everyday people" we see on television is but one small indicator among many that the world our own stories are being worked out in has changed.

These two aspects, global identity and the loss of family, typify the urban culture of North America more than almost any others of which I am

---

[6] For more on this see Jared Looney and Seth Bouchelle, *Mosaic: A Ministry Handbook for a Globalizing World* (Urban Loft Publishers: Skyforest, CA, 2017), 35-40.

aware. The fact remains, though, that most of our church programs are still designed around family units, segmented around linear stages of life, with language and images drawn from mostly white and mostly rural or suburban experiences. This may be one of the reasons so many of my friends struggle to connect with churches: the programs or events they have been asked to participate in were not bad, in themselves, they were just built for a context which is not "of the lost" (by which I mean not of these members of the Lost).

Conclusion

The Lost of today's urban America are an increasingly diverse and global community of which little can be said by way of generalization. However, when we begin to learn their stories, we do find a few points of commonality which can help us in our efforts to sow seeds and help harvest for the Kingdom. These elements include the importance of discovery, the binary relationship (both ignorant of and "knowing") of being only acquainted with Christianity, the need to treat discipleship as a process rather than an event, and the changing ethnic and familial makeup of the communities of which the Lost are a part. Let us keep these elements in mind as we begin the real task at hand: trying to reflect on a theology for this context.

Chapter 2

What Makes a Theology?

I feel both a certain trepidation and a certain arrogance claiming to be writing theology. It seems like such a lofty aspiration. The theological task, however, is one that none of us who serve Christ's church can avoid, so let us define what is meant by theology, here, before we move onto practicing it. In my studies, my favorite definition of theology comes from Robert Scharlemann. At the end of his book, *The Being of God* he says the following,

> *Theology has the task of inscribing "God" upon all names, "God is" upon all events, and "God is God" upon all identities. In carrying out that task it has the intention of speaking the truth so that the truth may be seen or heard. Sometimes it will be successful, and sometimes it will not succeed in this effort. It is free to acknowledge its failures as well as its successes, and to allow its assertions to be open to experimental testing. On occasion it must risk using language other than "God," and discourse about God, in order to say what it has to say, but even so its responsibility is for theological language. For the sake of truth, theology has to answer for the word "God," the tale "God is," and the judgement that "God is God." But it does not have to answer for God, the be-ing of God,*

and the identity of God, which answer for themselves when they answer.[7]

If we cut through the eloquence and the density of language, here is how I would interpret Scharlemann's definition with respect to the present discussion: we, in ministry, cannot help but talk about God. In simplest terms, this is precisely what theology means: "to talk about God." And when we talk about God, we are often wrong in what we say - sometimes totally wrong and sometimes partially wrong - but that does not prohibit us (or exempt us) from talking about God. And this talking about God, who God is and the implications thereof, is the task of theology. When we are doing this talking, it is for the sake of putting into words for ourselves and for others the experience of the one who is True but is beyond any ability we have to fully articulate. And that is okay. We can acknowledge our failures and our limitedness to speak in a way that completely captures God, because we are not responsible for speaking *for* God. Only *about* God.

So, by way of example, I respond strongly to the image of God as a father. I have a good relationship with my father and when I apply some of those attributes to God, I come to a greater understanding of who God is and what God might want for me as "a son." But when I use that language with Juan, it may lead him further away from a comprehension of God. Juan's family moved from Puerto Rico to escape an abusive father. He then had a series of fathers from his other siblings, all of whom abandoned the family, except one whom he loved but who was tragically murdered. Juan's only genuine memory of his own father was as an adult when he called Juan totally out of the blue to ask for money for an operation.

Juan may know what a father is. He, in my opinion, has been a good father to his own children. But Juan does not know how to relate to God as a father in a way that brings about a meaningful understanding about the

---

[7] Robert P. Scharlemann, *The Being of God: Theology and the Experience of Truth* (Seabury Press: New York, NY, 1981), 183.

character of God. To speak about God in a manner which distorts the Truth of who God is: this is a failure of theology. When ministering to others, to rely too heavily on theological language that we feel *should* be true - but in a particular context is distorting - is to fail to realize that God's being is not limited to any particular image or articulation.

Or, as another example, we might take the kinship language used among the church in the New Testament. The "framily principle" operating among my friends, perhaps counter-intuitively, makes this apt theological language for articulating what God-initiated community is like: that the church is one family, that Christ is like the first born, and we, as disciples, are all brothers and sisters not over one another but serving each other - this language makes better sense in my current situation than many churches I've seen in other contexts. One reason for this is that coming to faith sometimes puts my friends at odds with their families, who may not wish to see the transition taking place in the life of their loved one. One of the great difficulties in our team's work is when families tell new disciples "you can't change, we know who you *really* are." For reasons such as these, it is not uncommon for church to become a closer and more supportive community than family, and the language in Scripture affirms this reality.

Contrast this experience with what I have observed in other American contexts. In some places it seems that a church's primary concern must be fostering and serving the nuclear families which make up its membership. If the church relationships begin to take precedence over family ties, those same families might find a more "family friendly" church to be a part of. In this instance, the church exists not *as* my family but *for* my family. And this makes the familial language of church inaccurate in its application. As I have said, however, in my context it makes absolute sense that the church community becomes a family for the Lost, perhaps one with even deeper intimacy and loyalty than to their own kin. By using familial language in this instance, then, theology's task is better accomplished because the language points more truly towards the reality it seeks to describe.

So how do we go about this task of articulating a theology for a Post-Christendom context? I have asked myself this question incessantly throughout the preparation for this book and the best way I know, as is common in my work, is to tell a story: in this case of my landlord. Let us call my landlord Saul. Saul is in his early eighties and several years ago suffered a stroke which has limited his moments of lucidity considerably. Saul moved from Czechoslovakia to the Bronx shortly after World War II. His family was killed in the concentration camps and, while not generally practicing his Judaism in any formal religious manner, Saul, his wife, and their children have held strongly to their ethnic Jewish identity. One day on my way to get the mail I stumbled across Saul engaged in an argument with his Haitian nurse, James. "You!" Saul yelled at me, "You're the Christian, yes?" I realized I had caught Saul at one of his rare moments of clarity and, as he is generally a nice man, I did not want to miss the opportunity to speak with him. I stopped and affirmed that I was, in fact, "the Christian." "James wants to know why Israel and Palestine are fighting. Explain to him." This was not the last time I have regretted showing kindness to a neighbor.

"Well, James," I tentatively began to explain, "in the Bible, God called on a family that would grow to be the people of Israel and told them that he would give them that land if they would be faithful to the covenant he made with them."

"So, you're saying the land belongs to the Jews," Saul interjected.

"That's not what I'm saying," I replied.

"Oh! So, you're saying it belongs to the Palestinians!" Saul responded, too aggressively for my comfort.

"I'm not saying that either," I replied.

"Well tell James who it belongs to, then." It is these kinds of nuanced and highbrow cross-cultural engagements which make me proud to be a resident of the Bronx.

"Well, James," I began again, "in this covenant God made with Israel, the purpose was for them to bless all of the other nations of the world. And one of the ways God told them to do this was by treating the immigrant and the foreigner living among them with the kind of hospitality which they would show their own people. This was one of the conditions for God giving them the land. So, if the land does belong to Israel, I think we will know it by the way they treat the Palestinians living there."

"That's a good answer, Christian," Saul told me. Then I thanked him and hurried to get the mail.

The point of my story is this: I am going to have to talk about God and about what I think God is doing in order to "do" any theology here. I intend to do this through reflecting on certain passages in Scripture that I think are particularly relevant to the theological questions which have proved central to my ministerial context. And, as acknowledged in Schlarmann's definition, I am liable to be wrong or at least partially wrong in what I say about God. I hope that the criteria for judging the appropriateness of my theological assertions will be whether or not, when you try to put this into practice among the Lost, it adequately points them towards the deeper Truth that is the being and identity of the living God.

But I tell the story of Saul to make a deeper point. If you are reading this book without seeking to better form relationships with your neighbor, or without trying to participate in a conversation about how the church might speak more truly about God with those in a post-Christendom culture who do not share our faith, then I am not sure that what follows will be of much help to you. Moreover, if in these pages you seek easy answers to apologetical questions or a deconstruction of existing theological models, then please allow me to say that you need read no further. This book is neither an attack on nor a defense of any particular orthodoxy.

The realities I wish to speak about in the remainder of this book are as difficult to articulate as God is in God's own self. That is to say, I am trying to do theology. And theology requires one to try and articulate the

33

ineffable and to discuss the One whose first language is silence. This task is further complicated by the fact that it is not only the transcendent and mysterious God of the scriptures which I am seeking to speak about but it is the relationship of this God to culture - which is an almost equally fluid and inexpressible reality, and one I will just as surely, at times, miss the mark in trying to describe. All of this is to say that we are dealing with very difficult questions here and I ask that you have grace with me in the undertaking of it. I would ask that you not be like Saul, my landlord, on this journey. In the pages which follow I am going to make a number of claims to which it would be easy to respond, "So you're saying..." But I very well may not be saying whatever it is that you might be anxious about.

For example, I am going to discuss the ways in which created human institutions function as principalities and powers. One might respond, "So you're saying you don't believe in spiritual warfare?" That is not what I am not saying, as I hope you will see. Or it may be easy to read the sections in which I speak about forming others through the spiritual disciplines and prayer practices which come out of my own contemplative life and to respond, "So you're saying you have to be a mystic to disciple the Lost?" And I am not saying that either. I am also going to try, as I have in other works,[8] to use the language of myth to talk about Christian beliefs and about some aspects of scripture. I am not saying, perhaps, what you might think I am saying when I use such terms or make such claims.

My request is that you be patient and let me elaborate on many of the things I *am* trying to say, and give me the benefit of the doubt that I may actually be trying to be rather limited in what I argue. My reflections here will by no means answer all questions, eliminate all ambiguities, or address all the connected issues to those subjects which I do choose to address. I would, again, like to appeal to Jesus' own pedagogy. My method, rather than a more classical line of theological argumentation, will be to suggest what I think a theology for an urban and post-Christendom context might "be like."

---

[8] Looney and Bouchelle, *Mosaic*, 24-35; 145-150.

Jesus, in my reading of the gospels, spends very little time saying directly who God "is" and what God's Kingdom "is." He does, however, spend a great deal of time describing things that God and God's Kingdom are "like." The kingdom is *like* a mustard seed, God is *like* a shepherd with a lost sheep. Finding God's Kingdom is *like* stumbling upon a treasure in a field. If you want to come to Jesus you must be *like* one of these little children. Jesus tells us a lot about what God is like, but does not seem to spend much time worrying about a response of "So you're saying..."

I am boldly and, perhaps unsuccessfully, going to undertake a similar task with respect to my current context. For the remainder of this work I will look at three classic categories of theology: Anthropology (What is being human *like*?), Christology (What is Jesus *like*?), and Theology (What is God *like*?). I will examine each of these categories to address the ways in which I perceive current shifts in culture to have "remodeled the campus" of urban North American ministry, and to offer some insights into how we might begin to describe what being human is like, what Jesus is like, and what God is like. And it is my hope that, at the end of all this talking about God, I have pointed more truly to the reality of God in a way which helps us to reach the Lost.

For those students of systematic theology, you may notice that I am choosing to work in the reverse order of what is a common theological progression. Many thinkers begin with the question of who God is, then build on that foundation to talk about how this shapes who Christ is and then what humanity is. I have found, however, that for reasons both epistemological and relating to emotional processes, the more helpful starting place with the Lost is to establish a common vision of what it means to be a human being. I am deeply convicted that it is only when we are intimately concerned with the actual being and lives of real people that we can say we are constructing a theology grounded in love, which is the very nature of God. As I hope to demonstrate in the following section, when questions about our nature and being as human persons are left unaddressed, it is quite difficult for us to understand or to have interest in the divine. This is because I only understand God from the perspective of a human person. And I only understand nature and reality from the perspective of a human person. So, if we do not begin with a shared definition of what it means to be a human person, then we will not be capable of moving forward in theological dialogue until this has been established.

Additionally, it may seem strange for me to work from Christ back to God. This, too, is intentional. From my study of the history of Christian theology it seems that the identity of Christ has generally been contingent upon the identity of God. And to most of us who were raised in the church this seems not only appropriate but necessary. Often in doing theology, the qualities of God have been taken for granted - omniscience, omnipotence, omnibenevolence, omnipresence, eternality, preexistence - and the question which drove theological dialogue was, "How much like God is Jesus of Nazareth? How divine is he?" This seems to me to be the traditional Christological method from the church fathers through the more recent quests for the historical Jesus.

In my context, however, the word "God" is no longer pre-programed with an agreed upon meaning. Our larger American culture, including many who seemingly speak for the church, appears primarily to worship the God of Alcoholics Anonymous - God however you conceive of God - if they believe in any god at all. And many of the Lost, contrary to popular belief, do very much believe in a god. They just do not believe in the God of the Bible. And because they frequently do not see the Bible as an authoritative revelation above their own experiences of God, they are at an impasse when it comes to determining "who God *is*" and must settle for the question: "Who is God to me?" Many of the Lost do, however, have a high regard for Jesus and seem to implicitly trust that what they see in the Scriptures is a true revelation of him. The method in this work, therefore, will be to begin with

Jesus and work not towards the classical question "How divine is Jesus?" but the inverted inquiry, "How Christlike is God?"

In a context where so many feel betrayed by God, abandoned by God, unknown by God, or in which God is treated primarily as a spiritual anesthetic or a placebo to help one overcome difficult emotional experiences, we desperately need to establish some foundation from which we can begin to investigate the character of God. If, then, as Christians have confessed, Christ is the clearest self-revelation of the living God, why can we not begin with the person of Jesus and see if we cannot discover in him the character of this God who seems so otherwise unknowable or, to others, so radically inconsistent in identity? Humanity to Jesus to God - this will be the method I pursue for the current work.

On Orthodoxy

One of my favorite college professors was fond of saying that "the opposite of a true statement is a false statement, but the opposite of something profoundly true is often something else profoundly true." I would like to submit this as the best definition I know of orthodoxy.

The great doctrines of our faith are held in tension between two often seemingly irreconcilable poles, not unlike a theological tightrope. We might ask, for example, should the people of God be invested in the world or reject the world?[9] And the orthodox answer appears to be yes to both. We serve a God whose primary means of mission is the radical statement of the incarnation. God became like us. God entered our world and was subject to its realities and hardships. God even seems to enjoy and take delight in the created world. God in Jesus embraced culture, embraced language, embraced history, all for the purpose of revealing to us God's own nature and heart. And we are called to "become all things to all people" in order to

---

[9] By "the world" I mean the various secular (sub-)cultures and institutions which have been created outside of Judeo-Christian religious bodies: this being the common sense in which I hear "the world" being used by people of faith who were raised within Christendom and who are seeking to engage the context in which I work.

reach them with the gospel. This is a deep investment in and solidarity with the world. And yet we are also called to reject the world. To resist its allures, to not participate in its petty power plays, its idolatry, and in its systems of domination and oppression. We are called to prophetically protest as it tries to define our notions of love, of kinship, of completeness, and of desire. This is a deep rejection of and withdrawal from the world. It takes both of these poles to hold in tension the orthodoxy of Scripture.

Maybe another example is needed. Is Jesus fully human, or fully divine? The orthodox answer, of course, is: yes to both. But many of the great Christological heresies of history have been the result of refusing to hold these two seemingly opposite and profound truths in tension. Heresy is almost always a tremendous failure of imagination: it is the inability to believe that profound truths might be able to coexist in a way which appears utterly mysterious to us as human beings. But I would argue that we must hold these truths in tension or we will have no rope upon which to walk, and then we will fall - our theologies will cease to successfully reveal Truth so that it may be seen and heard. It is my hope that I will manage to hold in tension the truths which I seek to speak about in this work. It may be the case that on a few subjects I only address one side of a particular tension, but please trust that I am not trying to let go of the other side. I find that it is often the case that one of the poles has been neglected and is in need of some attention, but this is not a rejection of the truth of the opposite pole.

When both ends of the question are profoundly true, the primary theological project is not then to establish truth but to determine wisdom. Is Jesus fully human or fully divine? Yes. But which needs to be rediscovered in our context? Are we called to be invested in the world or reject the world? Yes. But how are we failing to do these both in our world? Is God radically immanent or transcendent? Yes. But how do we begin to relate to such a God today? Is the cross the ultimate sacrifice which renders all further sacrifices unnecessary because it has appeased the justice of God? Is it the ultimate revelation of love by a God who we would otherwise only see as capable of condemnation? Or is it the defeat of death and the revelation of a God whose faithfulness knows no cosmic limit? Or is it a divine trojan horse, unmasking the false myth of the scapegoat and so unseating the principalities and powers? Or is it a profound statement about a humanity so fearful and so blinded by idolatry that they would kill their own God on charges of blasphemy? And the answer, it seems, is yes. But what are the implications for imitating Jesus in taking up *our* cross for the communities in which we minister?

The theological task is not to drift to one pole or another, but to be able to stand within the tension which the various perspectives and experiences of scripture's authors and the church have set before us. Our work, in developing a theology of post-Christendom, is to demonstrate how to go about the tightrope walk which exists between the historical community of faith and our own contexts. This to me seems to be the nature of orthodoxy.

On Myth

In my last book, *Mosaic*, which I co-authored with my good friend and coworker Jared Looney, we spent a great many pages trying to reclaim the essential human category of myth.[10] I will not take up nearly so much space attempting the same here. I would, however, like to continue to use the language and the category of myth in this work. This seems to me to then warrant, at least briefly, a definition.

Myth has gotten a bit of a bad rap in the last century or two. People seem to invoke the label as if it means fairytale, or childish fantasy, or a category of thought that only the uncritical and the "pre-modern" mind would consider authoritative. This belittling of myth is not only naive - it is dangerous. And it is sad. The mythical exists in myriad expressions across all cultures and all of history. Myth is a way of articulating and preserving meaning which is so fundamental to the human experience it can at times be

---

[10] Looney and Bouchelle, 24-35.

difficult to differentiate from other forms of truth-telling. Perhaps this is why many "modernists" have been so hard on myth: they may simply not have realized how strongly myth is operating in their own world.

For the purpose of this discussion, I would like to frame myth in the following way: Myth (or the mythic) is the attempt by a particular cultural community to express something which is perceived to be profoundly true about Reality but difficult to articulate in another manner. Sometimes a myth is composed by a single person, but it is always preserved by a community who have accepted the myth as their own. A myth may be true, or it may be false. Its veridical status is not related to its status as myth. It is not myth because of its relationship to fact; it is myth because its function is to articulate a truth which might be inaccessible if pointed to in another form. Whether it successfully reveals Truth or not is also irrelevant. Because it has *tried* in this way to articulate a perceived truth about Reality, it is myth. Following this line of thinking we can freely admit, then, that there are both true and false myths. By which I mean that some myths may correspond with and reveal Reality, and some may not, but - true or false - they each attempt to do so.

Further, there are myths (both true and false in their nature) which appear to be based in historical events. In examining these events, we learn that at times they are accurate (in a historical sense) and at times they are based on historical fictions. When a myth presents itself as grounded in the literal historical events of our world, it is not important whether or not that claim is accurate for the myth to function as such. It will function as myth regardless of its historical validity, because its purpose was not so much to tell history as to reveal a deeper truth about reality.

For example, it is literally true that Abraham Lincoln was born in a log cabin on the frontier. It is true that he was a rail-splitter and a woodsman, was primarily self-educated in his pursuit of the practice of law, and that he became one of the most significant presidents in the history of the United States. These things are historically accurate. But when we memorialize and retell the myth of Lincoln, the historicity of the man is generally not what we are trying to convey. Insofar as we are speaking about the person - Abraham Lincoln - such as in a biography or a special on the History Channel, these elements may simply be facts and historical data. However, when we tell the story of Lincoln - in whatever truncated form (even simply the invocation of his name) - we are usually seeking to recall the myth of what we believe it is to truly be an American. We are stepping into a liturgical expression of the American mythology. We are calling on the myth of the self-made individual, the myth of honesty and integrity forged on the frontier, and the myth of the ability of a person of conscience to use power to create a more just society. These are basic myths which make up the mythic man: Lincoln. The fact that they align with historical facts does not take away from the way we are seeking to make them function: an expression of what we believe to be a deeper reality about our culture and identity.

Or as another example, in the following section I will examine how the initial chapters of Genesis function as myth. Some of my readers may at first be offended by this, but I am not telling you not to read the creation myth literally. You are welcome to read them that way; however, regardless of whether or not you read the Genesis accounts as historically literal, do read them as myth. They are an attempt to make a profound statement about the nature of the created order. If we miss this articulation - which I would argue is the purpose of their being recorded and preserved - in an attempt to establish the historical authenticity of the events which they describe, then we have not treated Scripture with what I would consider the appropriate authority. We have not done the discipline of discovering what the authors wish to reveal: the deeper truth about the nature of humans in the world, which is contained, not simply within the potentially historical details of the story, but within the myth.

The mythic can also be articulated through actions, symbols, and structures. A myth does not have to be in the form of a story. There are few figures in American society which better encapsulate myth than a judge. A judge always wears the same uniform, and these vestments are symbols which tell us something profound about the role of the wearer: that their function is timeless and impersonal, that they have put aside their own preferences and biases in order to stand in the place of the Law. We make judges the way we do because of their mythic function in our society. They are to sit in the seat of the power of Law. They are to discern for us what the Law will allow and how far its authority may be stretched. The judge is not meant to make the Law from the bench, nor render personal opinions about the Law. The judge speaks in behalf of the Law. She is an intermediary between the people and the Law. Is it any wonder that so many of our courthouses are built in the architectural style of temples? Our American justice system is built upon the myths we wish to construct and to articulate about the realities of order and law.

This is all the stuff of myth. These elements are created to articulate what we perceive to be profound Truths about reality. Sometimes we forget that, or we cease to notice it, but I would like, in these pages, to be able to speak about "the stuff" of myth. I would like to speak about it without people assuming I am claiming that many of their deeply held beliefs are false. I do not claim they are false; I am claiming they are myths. That, as I hope I have convinced you, is significantly different. Let me assure you that I have the highest respect for the mythic, especially as it informs our theologies. This is what makes it worth talking about.

Having established a method for moving forward, it is my hope that you keep in mind my concern in what follows both for orthodoxy and for myth. As we continue our tour of the post-Christendom context, I wish to examine the conflicting and profound truths which might help us address and speak faithfully about the questions at hand: What is being human like? What is Christ like? What is God like? And ultimately, how might we wrestle with these questions in a way which forms us as better witnesses to the good news of the Kingdom within our emerging context? In other words, let us try and do theology.

Section II

What Is Being Human *Like*?

Chapter 3

Our Place in the Order of Things

Then the Lord God formed man from the dust of the ground, and breathed into his nostrils the breath of life; and the man became a living being. And the Lord God planted a garden in Eden, in the east; and there he put the man whom he had formed. Out of the ground the Lord God made to grow every tree that is pleasant to the sight and good for food, the tree of life also in the midst of the garden, and the tree of the knowledge of good and evil...The Lord God took the man and put him in the garden of Eden to till it and to keep it. And the Lord God commanded the man, 'You may freely eat of every tree of the garden, but of the tree of the knowledge of good and evil you shall not eat, for in the day that you eat of it you shall die.' Then the Lord God said, 'It is not good that the man should be alone; I will make a helper as his partner.' So out of the ground the Lord God formed every animal of the field and every bird of the air, and brought them to the man to see what he would call them; and whatever the man called every living thing, that was its name. The man gave names to all cattle, and to the birds of the air, and to every animal of the field, but for the man there was not found a helper as his partner. So the Lord God caused a deep sleep to fall upon the man, and he slept; then he took one of his ribs and closed up its place

with flesh. And the rib that the Lord God had taken from the man
he made into a woman and brought her to the man. Then the man
said, 'This at last is bone of my bones and flesh of my flesh'...And
the man and his wife were both naked and were not ashamed.
-Genesis 2:7-25

I do not anticipate that humanity will ever construct a more perfect myth of the human person than the one we find in the first eleven chapters of Genesis. If nothing else, this helps convince me of its inspiration. The world, according to Genesis, was created, crafted even, methodically and intentionally by God without another order of things having preceded it. Readers of other creation myths will immediately note the difference here.[11] God does not subdue violence and chaos and force them into order. It is not from the bodies of the old gods or from the death of a previous cosmos that God makes this one. It is intentional, it is good, and it is organized, like the intention and organization of a garden.

At the center of this creation God placed a special work of imagination: humanity. And God did not simply make a man or a woman and put them there, because it is not good for a person to be alone. God saw that a person is not fully a person without a mirror and a partner. So God made them male and female - who are from the same flesh, and retain a degree of oneness even in their separate persons - and God placed them in the middle of what is perhaps the first divine tension, the first test of orthodoxy: the gulf between the created and the divine. This hierarchy was something like the following: God is at the top. God exists in God's own category and is without equal or peer. Below God is creation: all the plants and animals, the bacteria and the stars, the things that crawl on the ground and the elements hidden within the earth. But in between is the human, and the human is both creation and divine image. We have in us the nature of what is made, but also a reflection of the capacities of the one who made it

---

[11] By comparison I might suggest the Enuma Elish, Atrahasis, or Theogony by Hesiod.

all. We hold the tension between created and creator without fully feeling a sense of belonging to either. Or perhaps with a feeling of equally belonging to both.

In this original state, we were naked but that was all right. We did not seem insecure about that fact and we seemed to have very little to hide, to protect, or to obtain. And our first job was to name. This is one of our primary functions: to identify things, to find their purpose or meaning, to take stewardship of them, and to define them. This naming of the created world is a demonstration of our being placed over it, and it is an exercise of the authority which God placed in us. But we were not particularly cunning, and it took little suggestion for humans to let go of one side of the tension in which they had been placed. We wanted to know what it was like to be less limited; in Genesis 3 the serpent tempted us and we quickly chose to "be like God" (Gen 3:5) rather than to be satisfied with the limitations of our humanity.

In overreaching, we upset the balance of things. Through trying to "be like God" we discovered the crushing responsibility of having to be the source of our own provision and identity; this is how we discovered fear, insecurity, accusation, and betrayal. Overreach was how we discovered our nakedness and decided that we should be ashamed of it. Rejecting our own limitedness, our inherent dependence, we brought about the curse and the pain of autonomy: separation from God and the order of things.

In response to our overreaching the authority God had given, creation in turn overturned our authority over it. Life became inhospitable to life. Life now came at the cost of life. Competition and overreaching now defined what would survive and what would be the master of all. And this new order of things permeated out through the whole. In the chapters that follow the creation myth we see that this new order seeped into the family life and brother turned against brother (Genesis 4). It bled into the spiritual realm and the sons of God mingled with the daughters of humanity and created monstrous things which knew no limits (Genesis 6). Overreaching became the nature of human relationships and institutions as our ability to create and to name turned itself towards the creation of a great tower, so that we might corporately make a name for ourselves (Gen 11). Maybe in this way we would "be like God."

So, we ended up scattered. We ended up alone. Humans learned to cover over their nakedness through power and security. We learned to compete with and fear one another. We learned to extort, both each other and the creation we had been charged to care for. All in the name of becoming "like God." But in trying to become like God, we lost a sense of not only what God is truly like but what it was to be like a human. God gave us the power of definition, and we redefined the experience of living as a created person. And to reinforce our false sense of security and our power, we made idols, many of the very God who had created us. Perhaps we thought if we defined God in our own image then we would "be like God." This is the myth we find in the first chapters of Genesis. This is the story of what it is like to be human. And I think it is as true a description of our place in the order of things today as it has ever been.

This section is about what it is like to be human, so to begin I would like to draw out a few theological principles about the human experience which I think emerge from the Genesis myth. The first is that we humans are co-creators. We name things. We have the image of God in us and that has gifted us with a degree of God's creativity, God's imagination, and God's ability to make things which are not and to define things which are. The second principle is that we are in relationship. We are only fully human, it seems, when we are not alone. We seem to come to self-understanding and identity through our interactions with one another, with creation, and with God. One way to say that is that humans always need a mirror. Otherwise we do not know what we look like. The final principle I see in this myth is that we are naked: humans are limited, humans are weak, humans fail, and humans die. It is our very nature. In Genesis, God never had to take away our immortality, because God had never given us any to begin with.

Following the curse, we were simply cut off from the tree of life and that was enough to ensure we would not live forever. These three principles - creativity, relationship, and nakedness - define what it is like to be human. In this section, I will explore each of these three principles, considering how they operate in our context.[12]

---

[12] For the remainder of this work, "our context" will be used to refer to the post-Christendom urban context that is the area of theological focus in question.

Chapter 4

Makers and Shapers

I love the work of J.R.R. Tolkien. In fact, I have a rather large Tolkien inspired tattoo which takes up the better part of my right arm. I love his embrace of myth as a fundamental part of the human experience. I love his fascination with language as the primary foundation of building a world. I love how invested he was in song and art and ritual as integral parts of the expression of what it is to be created beings. I even like his distaste for allegory, which I tend to find didactic and uninteresting. And I think Tolkien's labor of love- the world he created - is, in many respects, a microcosm of the creative capacity in human beings which Scripture names "the image of God." Through myth, through language, through song, through art, and through the institutions and the systems we build, we are all - by virtue of the divine image - creators and shapers of our world.

Principalities and Powers

In my home, in the first years of my marriage, a group of us friends created a game we affectionately dubbed "Ugly Winged Horse." It combined many of the elements of our other favorite games with a few unique attributes which arose mostly from shared inside jokes and a desire to be irreverent in one another's company. It was great fun. We played almost weekly and, after the first couple of times we played, the rules never changed. We never wrote the rules down, there were no game pieces or required objects (besides paper and pen), it was simply a game founded on our collective imagination. This is actually a common attribute of human nature which I find surprisingly overlooked: by virtue of our creative capacity we like to play collective games of imagination. In fact, almost the entirety of world societies are built on an interlocking system of games which are the product of our collective human imagination.

Take economics, for example. Where does the worth of money come from? It comes from the collective agreement that it is worth what we say it is. When we begin, in any large numbers, to doubt the worth of the money - which we were previously pretending was worth something - the worth of the money does, in fact, go down. The rules of the game are the same for dollar bills as they were for wampum or the currency of giant stone discs used by the island people of Yap.[13] "But what about the gold standard?" a friend once countered when I was describing the collective game we call economics. "Yes," I replied, "and where does the worth of gold come from if not the shared game of attributing imaginary value to shiny objects?" Things are worth what we believe and can agree that they are worth, no more and no less. But by saying that economics is a game I am not saying it is not *real*. It is very real, as anyone who has had to pay back college loans can tell you. It is a game which shapes the quality of life for every human on this planet. Nevertheless, it is a game, simply a game of great scale and consequence.

On a lesser scale we might look at the games of social etiquette or grammar. The proper place setting for the salad fork is where it is because those are the rules. The reason you do not point with your foot in Thailand is because that is a part of how they play etiquette. The reason that Jared and *me* did not go to the store but Jared and *I* went there, is because the game of English is played that way. The changes in the game of gender in the English speaking world have begun to shape the rules of the language and it is now generally agreed that when speaking of "a person" in a sentence I can use the

_____

[13] Milton Friedman, "The Island of Stone Money," (*Working Papers in Economics*, No E-91 -3, 1991).

third person pronoun "they" rather than the more cumbersome "he or she" of yesteryear's grammar. It is all a game.

We might say the same of politics. Why is it a greater crime to kill a king than to kill a vagrant? Because we, as a group, have decided that the life of one is more valuable than the other. And why does one country begin at this river and end at that mountain range? Because the people living in that area have decided that it is so, and by force of collective imagination have defined that reality. And why does the winner of the election dictate the workings of the whole country when one out of every three people living there voted for someone else? Because those who voted for other candidates have agreed to abide by the rules of the game called democracy.

If I am at all convincing you about the gamification of human society, then the question we might ask is why we all engage in this collective play. Why don't the losers of the election stop playing? Why don't the poor decide the money of the rich is worthless and simply create their own "wealth?" Why don't people just decide borders don't exist, stop carrying little paper books with their picture and stamps in them - given to them by their mutually agreed upon overseers - in order to cross boundaries which only exist because they have, so far, agreed to believe that they do? And the answer, as best as I can tell, is because we believe that if we did not play these games the world would collapse into anarchy and violence. So, to prevent that chaos we give power over to these created systems in order that they might maintain stability and control in the world on our behalf.

I want to call out an aspect that I think is important about these games - these principalities and powers - if I can borrow the language of the apostle Paul: they may not be physical realities, but they very much exist. They are what I call psycho-spiritual realities. We may have built government buildings and hired bureaucrats to function as their representatives, but these systems primarily exist as entities in our collective imagination and therefore they exist in a non-physical realm from out of which they deeply affect us, they beg for our allegiance, and they often wind

55

up controlling how we see the world. Humans may create the powers, but we do not fully control them. And these constructed realities - like race, like country, like language, like time, like law - become the expressions and the channels through which we understand and engage the world and one another. They become the concepts by which we are limited in our coming to understand God and God's Kingdom (kingdom being one of these created realities which Jesus chooses to describe God's work as being "like").

I remember having a very enlightening discussion on the limitations of language with some friends in a Chinese church we started in Morningside Heights (Manhattan). "What is a word in Mandarin that doesn't have an English equivalent?" I asked. This is one of my favorite cross-cultural icebreaker conversations. "We have not been able to find the word you use to describe your parent's brother's children," one man answered. I told him we call them cousins. "Yes," he said, "but that is the same thing you call your parent's sister's children. We have different words for these things."

When it was my turn to give a word, I chose "nostalgia." I described it to them as the happy feeling that also produces longing when you remember things from the past. While intellectually they understood the wistfulness for something gone, they did not seem to fully relate to the nuances of emotion in the examples I gave for feeling nostalgic. Although it may have been due to my poor explanations, it seemed that they did not appear to have an equivalent word, and because the language game in which they were raised never created one, they did not deeply identify with the reality I was trying to describe. Language is one of the most important games we play, particularly when it comes to religion. It is also one of the most difficult to get hold of.

God has given us this power to name and to create, but most often the things which we imagine and we build seem to take on the very fallenness and overreach of the ones who created them. We might call this

Sin in its corporate or institutional manifestation.[14] The principalities and powers are often fallen to such an extent that, once established, humans as creators are not free to take hold of the reins once more; we feel enslaved to our own creations and we use them to oppress and to dominate one another. We feel certain that we cannot stop playing along without losing the small semblance of control we have over our world. Race, money, tribe, nation, etc.: we are locked within prisons of our own creation afraid to break free because the alternative appears to be chaos. To participate in the creation, perpetuation, and service of these principalities and powers is fundamental to the experience of what it is like to be human.

---

[14] We will return to this more in another section.

Chapter 5

Life Together

When I look back on my life thus far, it seems that there is not a period within my memory which was not filled with recurring bouts of loneliness. When I was a child, my family moved frequently. My older sister and I changed schools about every two years until high school; we moved towns and churches during pivotal seasons of our development. We learned very early what it's like to leave behind relationships, to enter a new context where you must begin completely anew, what it is like to return to the "old home" only to find that everything has moved on in your absence, to recognize the inevitable countdown until the people who you currently live among and define yourself by are no longer a part of your life. These were difficult lessons for a child, and they helped nurture my natural dispositions towards introspection, introversion, and melancholy. They were not, however, tragic or traumatic lessons. It is simply that I, from a younger age than some, discovered the inherent loneliness of what it means to be a human being in our world.

When I look back on my life, so far, it seems that there is not a period within my memory which was not filled with beautiful and refreshing experiences of intimacy. In every new town, we found new best friends and learned their life stories from before we entered them. We had a never ending stream of "adopted" aunts, uncles, and grandparents, who wished to give us their time, their attention, and their affection. We went through the experiences of having to join new sports teams and find new mentors and had the privilege of getting to practice developing those bonds again and again. These lessons were not unique to my growing up, but they did foster in me the importance of intentionality in relationship and seeking to develop vulnerability and intimacy. I learned from a young age the fundamental value of being known and of knowing others. This kind of intimacy is at the heart of almost every type of relationship and is an inherent part of what it means to be a human being in our world.

These two poles - intimacy and loneliness - make up the spectrum of the human experience. They are dual facets of our nature as relational beings. Everyone has experiences of intimacy and loneliness, to some degree, throughout the course of their life. And these experiences come to define our understanding of ourselves and our world. It is only in relation to others that we come to understand our experience of the world. In order to be alone, we must have the concept of being together. In order to feel close to another, we must have some notion of what it is to be separated. In order to interpret our feelings and thoughts, our hopes and fears, we measure in relation to those around us. As the Genesis account ingeniously recognizes, we are not what God created us to be when we are outside of relationship. People need one another in order to be fully human.

Mirroring

Every person is formed through a process of socialization. Being in relationship with others, engaging in dialogue, offending others and being offended, trying to repair damage when relationships are suffering - all these things constitute the means through which we come to form our egos and our external selves. When we tell a joke which we hope will win us attention only to find that it was disrespectful to someone whose opinion we admire, we see an aspect of our external self which we wish to change. So, we change. When we fall in love and we want the object of our affection to reciprocate, we try to discover the things they might like about us, and then project those things to them. When we discover someone we admire, we begin to shape our actions and opinions to reflect what we value in them. This is what it means to mirror in relationship.

I remember asking Juan once, "Why do you always tell your friends that I'm your pastor? It only makes everyone uncomfortable and I am just there to be with you guys." He shook his head and laughed. "You don't understand man," he told me, "People act different when you're around. I like to see that. I tell them so they'll change." And I realize that I do the same thing when I am with Juan's friends. I speak about Jesus, but I tone down the religiosity of my language. I tell the "edgier" stories from my life, not so much to impress them as to relate to them. I want to feel like I belong. I would be embarrassed if I felt like I was presenting myself as unable to understand them or identify with their experiences, even though that may actually be the case at times. When I see my reflection in interacting with them, I see qualities about myself - a propensity towards self-righteousness and a paternalism towards "the poor" - which I do not want to be a part of my external self. So, I try to adapt.

Juan's friends and I are mirroring to one another. We are using the ways in which we relate to each other to examine ourselves and to decide how we should be understood and presented. In the next chapter, we will talk about how mirroring relates to our sense of nakedness, but for now it is enough to note that mirroring is an important aspect of both intimacy and loneliness.

Intimacy Is Being Known

I have yet to meet anyone who does not wish to deepen their relationships with those they love. Despite having encountered some of the most misanthropic and belligerent people imaginable, there is still not a person whom I have met who would not - with those they are in close relationship with - like to be more known, more appreciated, and more loved. Human beings - as Genesis suggests - are hardwired to desire this kind of intimacy.

I speak about this often with KJ. For her, the ability to express herself in music is such an intimate and spiritual experience. She often talks about how connected she feels with an audience and assures me that it is not as creepy as I might suspect when fans feel a strong emotional affinity without having met her. This is just the nature of self-revelation. When we express a part of ourselves - through speech, through art, through physical affection - and it is accepted, we feel that we as a whole person are being accepted too. When we reveal ourselves and see the same elements are mirrored back to us in another, we find ourselves to be known and to be loved. This kind of mutual knowing and accepting seems to be the purpose of human relationship. It is the very definition of intimacy.

But our primary understanding of intimacy often comes through our lack of it. We want to tell our friend how much they mean to us and that we love them, but we do not want to be seen as foolish or weak. We deeply want to reveal the self-doubt and the insecurities we feel about our new job or our relationship with a significant other or about the upcoming move to a new city. But what if we are not supposed to feel that way? What if it is wrong: the way I feel, the things I am thinking? If I show myself externally the way I am internally, what if that person I am inside is not acceptable? What if that person is unwanted?

I am convinced that this basic insecurity is at the center of every person. Sometimes it is expressed in the need to meet others' expectations: there are those who are so afraid that they will fail to live up to the picture of themselves which they have presented to others that they cannot pursue intimacy for fear of not being good enough. There are others who are so desperate to be affirmed that they cannot say no to any requests or demands, because they believe that the only thing valuable about themselves is their utility to other people. For some people, no amount of praise or affirmation can ever convince them that at their core exists anything that is worthy of love.

And we cope with this dread in various ways which reflect our individuality. Some embrace eccentricity and reject "social norms," all the while feeling incredibly anxious and hoping that their protests will bring them the attention and affirmation they really desire. Other people seek out power and positions of authority thinking maybe if people have to depend on them they will come to see them as valuable and then love them. There are some people who withdraw into themselves and live almost entirely in their own fantasy worlds and imaginations. Perhaps, they think, if I do not interact with people, I will not have to reveal how plain and how unexceptional I am; I will not have to fear rejection because I am not "putting myself out there." Whatever the mind game, the desire is the same: people wish to be known, to be valued, and to be loved, but they fear that they are not.

The most pernicious aspect of the mind game, however, is that it begins to breed the very insecurities and self-hatreds which cause people to divide their projected self from their inner self. "If she knew how much I needed her to keep coming to me for counsel in order for me to feel validated, she would lose respect for me," the minister might think in her heart. "I cannot even consider the possibility of losing my spot as project manager, that's the only reason people in this office even talk to me," the young employee thinks. "I feel like I'm more into her than she is into me, she must feel like I'm pathetic," fears the boy after the second date. So, the person who is trying desperately to present an external self which will win them acceptance must redouble their efforts at projecting how they wish to be, for fear of being discovered needy and without worth. Nothing inhibits real intimacy like the effort to manufacture acceptance.

But what of real intimacy? Those times when we can take off the mask and be honest about our true feelings and hopes are special, perhaps, because they are so difficult. In my own disciple-making efforts, I often try to begin setting the culture for intimacy by making confessional statements at the start of new relationships. It can be awkward, but the effort is not (when I'm emotionally healthy) for the sake of being seen as "very authentic" - which would be just another projection of a false self by which I would hope to win love. These are genuine attempts to create a culture of self-disclosure. So, I will say things like, "I'm sorry that was a terrible exaggeration, I was just trying to sound more impressive." And then we can laugh about it. Or I might say, "That was a stupid thing to say, I was trying to be funny but now I feel embarrassed." Or, because I like to seem knowledgeable, I often have to come back around and confess, "I actually don't think I know almost anything about that thing you mentioned." And then the trajectory of the interaction has changed. Now rather than being anxious and trying to compensate for one failed bid for acceptance with another, the ploy has been unmasked. By revealing the fears which drive us to pretend, we actually find commonality and we discover the ability to create genuine intimacy.

This is where I think mirroring comes in. It is when we can look into another person in relationship and see the same insecurities, the same need to be accepted and to be loved, reflected back at us - it is when we see these things clearly mirrored that we are able (if we are being attentive) to recognize them in ourselves as well. And when we discover or confess them in ourselves, then we mirror for others and allow them to see how overwhelmingly normal it is to feel needy, to feel embarrassed, to feel inadequate, or to feel unlikeable. All too often, however, when we see the same fears and insecurities in others that we know to be in ourselves (although sometimes we repress or ignore that self-knowledge), our temptation is to judge, to reject, and to hate.

It is one of the great ironies of human relationship that the things which we are ashamed of and despise about ourselves are often the same things we also reject and judge in others. There is almost no person who is more judgmental and more incapable of intimacy than the person who

64

carries within themselves a deep sense of shame and unworthiness. But it is those people who are able to see their own blemishes, to admit their weaknesses, to humbly disclose them, and to risk the rejection and judgement of others who open the doors to truly establishing relationships with real love and genuine acceptance.

This has certainly been the case in Mary and Rebekah's community. It was through the difficulties of their first few years as a church that they began to create authentic relationships and develop their love for each other. Without their having to come to church angry, to come heartbroken, or to come guilty, to come apologetic - without their having to practice challenging one another's egos, and calling one another out on their unforgiveness - without these practices of Christian mirroring they would not have been able to create a community for truly broken and hurting people to find a home and the heart of God. If we do not create spaces where people can look within themselves and confess, without fear of rejection, that they may be lost, no one will ever be found.

I remember the first meeting we had of the church in KJ's house. Going around the circle and giving our spiritual biographies, one man said, "I believe in God, but we're not getting along right now." He went on to talk about the murder of a close relation which greatly impacted his family and his own subsequent battle with depression. He explained that he didn't want to believe in God, but he couldn't deny God. As he saw it, the only option this left him was anger. And to the credit of this group, nobody had any advice to give. Over the following months I saw my friend come to a stronger and healthier spiritual and emotional state, but he continued to reference that first meeting as what convinced him to persevere as a disciple. "This is really church," I recall him saying many months later. He confessed how healing it was not to need to pretend he was having a different experience of faith than was honest. The permission to be in process was the key to feeling known and supported to continue.

One of the things you may have noticed is that intimacy seems to come more readily out of shared weakness than shared strength. It is the vulnerable spaces - the fears, the dreams, the doubts, and the hopes - which are often the avenues to true intimacy. Rarely is there more insecurity and posturing to be found than in a room full of people who are at the top of their class (in whatever category that is). Equally rarely will you find communities more intimate than ones which have had to undergo great hurts and great failures together, but which have remained committed to transparency and forgiveness. The best avenue I have found for allowing this kind of intimacy to develop is in my relationships where I am open about my prayer life, but in order to talk about that we will first need to address being lonely.

Loneliness Teaches Us Love

Loneliness happens when the radio in the car breaks, so you have to make the road trip in silence. Loneliness happens when you come to the end of a moving novel and you look over in bed and your spouse is already asleep. Loneliness happens to the mother who arrives back at the hotel room on a business trip and wonders how her family fared for dinner. Loneliness happens to the child who arrives home before his parents are off of work, and he finds that there is nothing good on television. It happens to the immigrant whose mind is weary from thinking in a foreign language all day, but for whom there is no one to speak with in her native tongue. It happens to the new son-in-law who, at the end of the first night of the first Christmas with "the whole family," realizes how much of his bride's life history he is not a part of.

Loneliness is not social rejection and it is not a feeling of hostility towards others. It is the heartfelt intuition and ache over being separate from other people. It is a recognition of how truly and unutterably alone we are beneath our constant stream of stimuli and our incessant mental commentary. It is the recognition that we are not fully known, fully expressible, or fully possessing of the being of others. Loneliness is not a negative feeling. It is not a sign that there is something wrong with us. It is not something which we should attempt to avoid, although we can choose to do so. Loneliness is the experience of a profound truth: that each of us is more vastly unknowable and far more separated from one another than we often dare to admit. And it is in loneliness that we realize our deep need for intimacy and the great danger of relationship.

When we find ourselves alone, truly alone - in moments when we turn off the video playing on a loop in our mind's eye, and we quiet the commentators who live in our heads - when we embrace moments of loneliness for the genuine revelation that they are, it is then that we learn how frequently we do not treat people like people. When I get very quiet and very still there are feelings I discover which I spend most of my time covering over. There are fears. There is deep-seated grief. There are memories of hurt and of anger which I have been repressing which begin to play in an endless loop in my mind. I have thoughts about the future and about the present, doubts, concerns, and regrets which I would wish to share with someone, but there is no one to share them with who would be able to take them away.

When I am alone, I feel within myself the urge "to do something." To go out, to watch a movie, to lose myself in a book, to text a friend, to check my social media. I want to do anything to relieve the inexpressible pressure of not being connected to something. And this is not simply boredom. It is more urgent than that. It is emotionally heavier than boredom. This is loneliness. And it is here that I realize a deeply important facet of my humanity. I realize, in loneliness, that at the center of my being is a question, is a doubt. We can call it a void. And I realize that I wish to fill this void. I wish to fill it with noise. I wish to fill it with distraction. I wish to fill it with meditation or recollection or prayer. And most deeply, despite my own personal introversion and appreciation of solitude, I wish to fill this void with the love and the attention of other people. I wish to be with others, not because I love and want to give attention to them, but because I wish to fill up the void of doubt and of emptiness that I discover in myself when I am alone. I wish to use people as objects for my own gratification and self-care.

I would suggest to you that, with respect to this impulse, I am not alone. I would suggest, and perhaps hope, that what is true of my own heart is true of the human heart, itself. I would be so bold as to suggest that those who do not identify at all with the experiences which I am describing have most likely been avoiding true experiences of aloneness, regardless of how much time they spend outside the presence of other people. And it is the revelatory power of loneliness which makes it such a painful gift.

In the Genesis myth, with which we began this section, God says that it is not good for the man to be alone. Our culture has very clearly embraced this aspect of the creation story and has tried to foster constant social connection with ever greater frequency as the technology becomes available. We live in a world in which one must go to considerable effort to not be available. Ironically, during the rare moments when we cannot be reached, we often are anxious and fear that this will be the cause of a great misfortune in our lives. What if someone tries to call me? What if there is an emergency? In our culture it is expected that you apologize if you are not able at all times to respond to others' bids for attention through email, text, e-chat, phone call, Twitter, Facebook, and whatever other platforms for "connecting" we are liable to invent in the near future.

All of this connection appears to tell us that we, as people, are important. It seems to tell us that we are necessary and valued. One of the first thoughts which occurs to us when we feel lonely is, "I wonder if anyone has tried to contact me in some way?" The entire communications enterprise not only feeds our latent sense of narcissism but nurtures the ugly underside of self-centeredness: an overwhelming insecurity at the thought of losing other's attention. Herein lies the gift of loneliness. It is very important that, like Jesus, when we find ourselves in the midst of a crowd - particularly if the reason for their gathering is so that we may be seen and heard - we recognize that this is the time to retreat, to go to a lonely place, and to remember how easy it is for others to become the source of our sense of worthiness and the reason for our existence.

It is in loneliness that we learn that we are like other people. For both the proud and the poor in spirit, true loneliness reveals the same limited and separated sense of being which is at the center of us all. It is there that we learn to see and to recognize the weak and "untouchable" parts of ourselves which become the revelations that create intimacy. Loneliness teaches us not to be estranged from the insecurities and self-doubts in our hearts; it teaches us that shame and self-hatred exist within us and that we are in a constant mode of covering over these things when we do not allow ourselves to withdraw from the company of others. Loneliness shows us how badly we feel the need to be loved, and by accepting who we are when we encounter ourselves in that solitude, it teaches us how we might go about accepting others so that they may feel truly loved.

It is for this reason that loneliness is so critical to intimacy. Loneliness is mutually exclusive with intimacy in that one cannot at the same instant genuinely feel loving acceptance and alone. However, loneliness is not intimacy's opposite. Loneliness and intimacy are fundamentally dependent on one another. The individual who does not know what it is like to feel alone and to acknowledge the void within is constantly in danger of unknowingly using others to create for themselves a sense of worthiness or belonging. And the individual who will never disclose themselves with authentic vulnerability to others is the very same one who will attempt to generate a degree of mental activity so busy and distracting that they will never truly feel alone in solitude. Here, too, mirroring is important. It is critical that others, particularly the Lost, see Christians emulate Jesus by entering into and embracing experiences of loneliness as a fundamental part of the human experience. For if we cannot be alone, then we will not come to know our own weakness. And if we cannot know our own weakness, we will not truly find intimacy. If we are cut off from these basic experiences which are at the very root of the human person, then we will continue to live out the cursed life of people who remain naked and ashamed.

Sharing Prayer

As I mentioned earlier in the chapter, it is my experience that those relationships in which I am most open about my prayer life are the ones which become the most intimate. I hope at this point the reason for this phenomenon is obvious. My prayer life is built on a daily block of time spent being silent and alone. It is the intention of that practice to allow the space to be present to God and to create the interior silence which allows for me to hear God speak, if God wishes to do so. After almost a decade of daily practice, I can tentatively affirm that God does not often wish to do so. And in my first several years of contemplative practice, I was insecure about that fact. Very few "experiences" were coming out of prayer. I grew afraid that I was wasting my time. My spiritual director, however, encouraged me to sit through the feelings of aridity and boredom and because I respected him and wanted him to respect me, I did.

It is only in retrospect that I see the way God has used the long periods of silence in my prayer life to draw out in me those most broken elements of my heart. The great wounds in my interior life are, now, intimate acquaintances of mine. We met one another in a vast sea of loneliness. We now see each other regularly. These wounds come out when I get quiet and at times I begin to grow anxious because I start to feel the void emerge, and no one is making any commentary about it, and nothing is happening to make it go away, and I'm not avoiding looking into the void and seeing what is there. This kind of prayer is not generally very consoling, but it is absolutely essential for my continued sanity and ministerial health.

It is necessary because, in prayer, I am forced to recognize the neediness, and the loneliness, and the overwhelming insecurities which exist in my daily interactions with work and family and neighbors. I have to look within myself and confess how controlling and how manipulative I am in my relationships. I see my intense fear of failure and my need to prove myself as valuable and as competent in the eyes of those I respect. I find that out of the silence slinks the unsilenceable belief that I am not enough, will never be enough, and that everyone who sees me as I am will come to hate me and to reject me as much as I would almost certainly do to them if they were stripped so bare before me. And this is the final revelation: that I am unwilling to be to others the person I most desperately hope they will be to me. Love is not my being. I am not God. And this makes me feel naked and ashamed.

This is my daily practice of prayer, and in the name of intimacy I have made a concerted effort *not* to hide my prayer life from my friends who I have asked to follow along with me as we, together, search for God. I do not go revealing my innermost self to just anyone off the street, but it is not long into my relationship with Lost people before I begin to talk about what it is that God brings out of my interior silence. And the more I find that they are receptive to these disclosures, the more I reveal and the more vulnerability they offer in return.

Alan, KJ, Rebekah, Mary, Juan, and others, know with regularity the fruits which emerge - good and bad - from my time spent in prayer. I work very hard to disclose these with a genuine heart of humility and confession, because it is easy to reveal ourselves in the appearance of humility and in the appearance of being confessional when truly we are just wearing another mask which we hope will make those around us feel that we are pious and righteous and deserving of love. And it is also a strong temptation to put ourselves down before others, to appear vulnerable, all the while fishing for their affirmation and approval. This false humility is a kind of spiritual cancer in which the cells that should be healthy are death because they reproduce a mutation which chokes out life. So, I try very honestly to reveal, as responsibly as I can, the depth of my own lostness, my own loneliness, and my own desire to be known and to be loved. I find this practice often cleans off the mirrors between us: in my own disclosure, they see something of themselves and reflect those things back to me. I have found that this is the truest road to establishing intimate friendships and intimate churches. I have found, thus far, that this is the path to realizing the fullest experience of what it is like to be human.

It is only when we discover the inability of other people to fill the void within us that we can allow them to be who they are and not what we want them to be. It is when we allow people and things to fail in completing us (and ourselves to fail in completing others) that we are free to love them and to be loved to the fullest extent by others. But often it is easier to make an idol out of others and of God. It is easier to demand that they give us the experience of being known and loved which will dispel the emptiness at our center. And it is easier to make an idol of ourselves to project to others in exchange for love: a person without the fear and neediness that exists in us. This idolatry, however, prevents genuine intimacy. We cannot love or be loved by others unless we do the difficult work of coming to know and accept the *real* person, one who is lonely and hurting and cannot be everything which they might wish. It is not good to be forever alone, but it is out of our loneliness that we find the capacity to be in relationship with others in a way that love may prevail.

Chapter 6

Naked and Afraid

Reviewing the previous two chapters, I recognize that the theme of nakedness has already been addressed to a large degree. While this was not necessarily intentional, it seems appropriate for a couple of reasons. First, because I would be distrustful of any articulation of the human person which lent itself too easily to compartmentalization. Humans are complex beings and we are - at the same time - fully integrated beings; both of these aspects should be retained when we try to use the sort of artificially constructed categories I am employing here. Second, it seems appropriate because it is in understanding the previous two categories - our creativity and our relationality - that we begin to see the subtle ways humans try to cover our nakedness. We try to create systems and structures to cover ourselves. We use these powers to protect our small kingdoms from falling into chaos. And we use our relationships to cover ourselves. We make games to give us a sense of control. We make masks and projections and avoid loneliness to try to fill the void in which we discover our own vulnerability.

There are a number of reasons we feel the need to cover our nakedness. One is a fear of rejection. Each one of us has deep insecurity about being found wanting in some way. We are afraid that we are not smart enough, not beautiful enough, not rich enough, not righteous enough. Not adequate in some way which will cause others to pronounce us abject or unworthy. Another reason is a fear of being hurt. It requires a long and difficult process for wounds to heal, especially if the one who hurt us is a person from whom we expected love. When a spouse, or a parent, or a mentor, or a friend fails us or betrays us, we try to find ways to protect ourselves from being hurt again.

A third reason is the fear of hurting others. Many of us feel a malevolence inside: sometimes anger, for others it is envy, for some it is a chronic neediness in which they cannot stop using and abusing others. Those who recognize this inclination within themselves are often ashamed. They may hate themselves and wish to repress and hide it. The final reason is a fear of a sort of death: many of us have a sense that if the idolatry surrounding our identity were totally revealed - individually or corporately - we might discover that who we have believed ourselves to be has never existed at all. This spiritual death is one of the most painful of human experiences. We may often rather physically die than discover the degree to which we are not the persons we wish to be. We would often rather not go on living than to accept responsibility for the myriad failures, disappointments, and shame which are the lot of living in relationship.

Almost every person in the history of the world is afraid of this kind of death. It may appear to be merely physical death we fear but may more accurately be non-existence. We are afraid to be forgotten. Afraid to not matter to anyone, to have never mattered. Afraid to find ourselves weak and without the power to shape our circumstances. We are afraid that the actions which we have undertaken in our lifetime are pointless. That the things we have built will crumble. That the dreams we pursued were foolish. That if we are memorialized at all, it will be as failures, and the things we have acquired will rust and be thrown into the trash-heap. "Death" is the linguistic totem - the myth - we invoke when we try to point toward this much larger reality which we fear.

I would like in this chapter, then, to try and fill in more of this picture of our essential nakedness. I would like to add a few components to the model so that we might see some of the many subtle ways humans try to

74

cover themselves in our world. The variety of tools we utilize to do this is vast, and I have neither the expertise nor the interest to try and articulate them all. Therefore, I will only be looking, here, at three "coverings" which are particularly prevalent in my ministry experience: power, pleasure, and cynicism. Before I do that, however, I would like to briefly address how nakedness fits into a theology of Sin.

On Sin

Scripture and the theological tradition have developed a profound way of speaking about the common reality which emerges from our response to our own nakedness. They call it Sin. I remember a conversation Alan and I had one evening while we took my dog on a walk in the park near my apartment. As usual, we were sharing with one another about our practices of prayer. My practice is rooted in the Christian contemplative tradition and his emerges from his study of Zen Buddhism. We often trade books and insights with one another and this frequently leads to fruitful discussions about God and about the human spirit.

This particular evening, I began to talk to Alan about the ways in which God reveals to me the Sin which is so entrenched in my heart. In my life, prayer is often a very purgative experience, as I mentioned in the last chapter. In prayer I have to hear God speak truthfully about the Seth who is loved by Christ. The reason this is painful is because I do not particularly love that Seth, myself. It is painful because I have to recognize that it is only when I am able to accept the person who I am - a man who is deeply scarred by Sin - that I am being the one whom God loves. God does not love the man who I wish to be and who I project to other people. God loves the man who I truly am. I must accept this identity if I wish to participate in the love which is given by God.

As I shared these thoughts with Alan he asked if I would elaborate on what I meant by Sin. Sin is not - to my knowledge - a central aspect of Zen teaching, and most of what he had heard Christians talk about as sins were specific actions of bad behavior for which they wanted to be forgiven. How is it that God could forgive something as fundamental and existential as what I was calling Sin? The answer I gave, though hopefully less formal, was along these lines.

Within all of us there is the interior person, what I was referring to as "the man who I am." This is the being that exists underneath the ego, the rational mind, the projected self, and the caprice of human passions; it is also the person who encompasses those things. This is not the narrator in our heads; this is whoever it is that is listening to that voice. It is a part of ourselves so basic that many of us never recognize it even exists, thinking that our thoughts and our feelings are what make us "us." Whether or not this is what scripture means when it talks about the soul or the spirit, I do not know, but this person is at the center of the awareness we seek to cultivate in silent prayer. Alan confirmed that up to this point his experience of prayer aligned with what I was describing.

I continued. It is the very nature of this person which I think Christ seeks to transform. Obviously as this transformation takes place the ego, the emotional life, and the thought and behavioral patterns are changed as well. These outward manifestations are what most people are focusing on when they talk about sinning. But it is the brokenness at the heart of our true self which is the origin of these things. It is that part of ourselves which makes us choose destruction - of relationships, of our bodies, of creation - which I would call Sin. Our sinful thoughts, sinful feelings, sinful actions are the manifestations of this internal reality called Sin. The outward things must be forgiven, because they hurt and destroy in the realm of relationship. But the inward reality must be redeemed. It must be saved. It must be healed and made more like Christ. Although I realize this explanation sets aside the issue of Sin as a corporate reality (which I addressed in our discussion of principalities and powers) this seems like a more honest and more holistic theology of Sin as a personal reality.

This Sin, which is at the heart of each one of us, is the tree which bears the bad fruit of our nakedness. It is the root of the brokenness we institutionalize in the principalities and powers we create. Sin is this fractured perspective and deep woundedness which causes us to choose the very things which - even as we choose them - we know will only lead to death. It is the tragedy which plays out within us all and creates the fear of rejection, the fear of being hurt, the fear of hurting others, and the fear of death. Sin is what we see clearly when we embrace loneliness. This is part of the nakedness we seek to cover over. I believe this is the sense in which Jesus was "without Sin." And this is the reality which God wishes to redeem.

Reflecting on the urban post-Christendom context in which I work, I would argue that - among the many theological frameworks in need of repair - none is probably more critical than our theology of Sin. In academic terms we would call it "hamartiology." So many of my friends among the Lost are rejecting of and almost entirely allergic to the language of Sin. While it might be easy to ascribe this to feelings of guilt or a desire to avoid admitting their dependence on God and need for grace, such explanations do not reflect their actual theological thinking. Well before any of our groups had any committed or baptized "converts," almost every one of my friends identified a deep brokenness within themselves and a deep desire to be made whole, to encounter God, and to find a sense of healing and fullness in following Jesus. It is not the experience of Sin they find objectionable but the language and frameworks which they have encountered in the church: our primary hamartiologies typically having been built around medieval concepts of honor and sovereignty which make little sense in our current context.[15] For many of the Lost these theological frameworks make little sense out of their actual experiences of pain and which have been used - from their perspective - to induce feelings of shame and guilt without offering any apparent

---

[15] For more on this see Stanley J. Grenz, "Theology for the Community of God" (Eerdmans Publishing Company: Grand Rapids, MI, 1994), 342-345.

solutions that resolve the actual woundedness and alienation that drew them to Jesus in the first place.

This is, I think, a fair critique. And for this reason, I have seen ministries and disciple-makers work to retire or set aside the language of Sin in order to better contextualize their message. While an understandable decision, this seems an inadequate solution. If we, as Christians, really hold the conviction that all have sinned then why would our hamartiologies not be the most relatable aspect of our theology? If we cannot speak in our context, with the language of Scripture, about our own woundedness in ways which are eminently relatable, then in what sense can we say our theologies reflect an authentic experience of what it is like to be a human being? The fact that what we claim as a most universal of human experiences - Sin - is utterly foreign to the Lost in our context is not the failure of those outside the church to see the truth of our beliefs. It is a demonstration of how anemic our own conceptions of Sin have become and of the need to reorient ourselves as to how this language might better point us toward the reality of human life and community as it is articulated in scripture. With that in mind, I would like to turn our attention to the ways that, in our culture - among many other things - God wishes to redeem us from Sin by saving us from our struggle for power, our destructive quest for pleasure, and our embrace of an abiding cynicism.

The Struggle for Power

My friend Rez is a wizard. I met him one evening when I went over to Juan's house for a Bible study. He was smoking on Juan's stoop, so I sat down and we started talking. Juan has long had a habit of taking young drug dealers, convincing them to sell out, and then paying them to work odd jobs in his auto-shop until they have enough experience to find legitimate employment on their own. Rez, it turned out, was the latest in this line of young men. He worked at the shop for a few months, during which time we would occasionally converse. He routinely sat in on my Bible studies and spiritual conversations with Juan, and after a few months he moved to Kentucky to begin a vocational placement program there. About six months after moving, however, Rez hurt his back and had to return to New York while the doctors decided how to begin rehabilitating his injury. It was during this time that I learned about Rez's training as a wizard.

When Rez moved back to the Bronx he was staying with his father, who, it turned out, lived on the same block as me. Rez was bored and lonely, and he had some unresolved grievances with a gang in our neighborhood, so he would call or text me many afternoons and we would walk up to safer territory and hang out. He informed me that during his previous time in the Bronx he had lived with a roommate who taught him what he refers to as "godstuff." Godstuff, as Rez explains it, is like this: human beings have all kinds of powers that we have forgotten - the power to manipulate things with our minds, to see into people's thoughts, and to bend people's actions to our will. When we learn how to access these powers, we rediscover the truth about ourselves. We rediscover that human beings are like gods. Sound familiar?

Rez was quick to assure me that we are not God (who Rez believes in, alongside most of the deities of the Greek and Norse pantheons, as well), but we have the power of lesser gods. "It's like Hercules," he explained. Rez's roommate learned these secrets through consultation with the spirits of the dead, and he taught Rez how to summon demons, to speak with the dead, and how to use these powers to get what he wanted from others. In the time that I knew him, Rez primarily used his training to get people to give him money and to get women to sleep with him. He swore that if he could manage to touch you, that through this contact he could make you agree to do what he wanted. Rez was hesitant to use his powers often, however, because he had begun to hear voices speaking to him and trying to pull him further into the spirit world. On more than one occasion he claimed to have slipped into something like a fugue state and lost track of who he was and what he was doing. He was well aware that the powers he was tapping into were borrowed, and they could turn on him.

It may not surprise you to know that in my time in seminary we did not spend a lot of time studying how to disciple people like Rez. One of my favorite things during our time together, though, was when I would show up at Juan's house and Rez would ask, "Is it time for church?" Regardless of what I had intended to come over for, the answer was now "yes." Rez loved to interpret Bible stories. He has given me my favorite exegesis of the story of the Gennesaret demoniac in Luke 8. Juan, Rez, and I read the story together one afternoon at the bar. At the end of the story I said, "One of the things that has always confused me about this is why the townspeople were afraid of Jesus and asked him to leave. If they were afraid of Legion, why weren't they pleased that Jesus had healed him? Rez, you know more about dealing with demons than I do, what do you think?" This is a pretty normal way I try to bring discovery into studying Scripture with others.

"Well," he answered, "there's two things you need to know to understand the story. One is that demons are not supposed to mess with animals. Animals are pure, because they don't have souls, and when they get possessed, they go crazy. You never try to practice godstuff on animals." He gave me a look that suggested I was supposed to affirm that this was correct. "The second thing is that all those people who were living in the town, they may have not been possessed like Legion, but they use the spiritual world to get what they want in life just like everyone else. Why would they want Jesus to stay around if he has the power to take that away from them?" Clearly, Rez knows something very profound about the nature of power and its place in the human experience.

My world, by virtue of the global people groups I work among, is filled with practitioners of spiritualism and folk religion. Sometimes it is Santeria, sometimes it is "godstuff," sometimes it is the magical practices of folk Islam which are prevalent among my Bengali friends. Other times it is the health and wealth gospel, which is a sort of contemporary folk-

Christianity. I have many friends among the Lost who, when times get hard, begin to bargain with God and find ways to get God to fulfill their wishes. The practice of planting "financial seeds" for a divine return on investment is quite common among the nominally Christian individuals in my life. Even among my most "secular" friends, astrology and totems for good luck are normal elements of their lives. Everyone wants access to the power of the spiritual realm. Maybe I cannot be like God, but that does not mean I cannot try to bend God (or some lesser power) to my will. And the things these powers are used for are the ordinary everyday trials of human life: money problems, health problems, relationship problems, etc.

So, my friend Isabel might go to the *santero* in order to put a curse on whoever put the curse on her daughter which made her get sick. Or my friend Muhammad will put a verse from the Koran in large letters on the wall of his new business, to ensure God makes it successful. When my friend Finn was a child, his grandmother once took his sleepshirt to the "wise woman" who lived in the mountains to have her bless it, so that he would stop being haunted by demonic nightmares. These type of spiritualist practices exist in every culture and they make up a large percentage of life for many people.

I once asked Juan how it was that he could say his family was not religious when they were so obviously immersed in the practices of Santeria. "You don't get it." He told me, "That's old Spanish magic. It isn't a religion; it's just the way things are." This is how he explained to me the perspective of many Christians globally who continue spiritualist practices after their conversion. From Juan's perspective, they are not betraying their faith, they are supplementing it with something that solves the problems they believe religious faith will not. Whether it is couched in the beliefs of a codified tradition or "it's just the way things are," the root of these practices is the same. At the end of the day these are ways of seeking power in order to cover our own nakedness. These practices are a means of attaining security from pain and death. They are attempts to control our circumstances. It is human to seek out such powers.

"But what of 'modern' cultures?" someone might ask. "Haven't we evolved beyond those superstitions?" I would answer that we have evolved in the way that all evolution takes place: we have adapted in order to continue the same life in new environments. We have not transcended. To give us a sense of security, we have embraced the magic of pharmaceuticals and of financial markets. To attain control over our circumstances, we may seek out positions of authority, or we try to make friends with those who already have them. To quiet our fears, we search after the latest possessions and experiences to establish a lifestyle which will be seen as valuable or, better, enviable by others. It may be political capital instead of spirits, the stock market over the Botanica, and elective surgeries rather than magic rituals, but we have not transcended our fear of death and pain. We have not evolved beyond our pathological need for security and control. We have merely adapted. Regardless of culture or historical context, it is deeply human to feel naked due to a lack of power.

The Quest for Pleasure

At the beginning of church we always go around the table and everyone shares something they are thankful for from the last week. Then we go around the table again and everyone shares a need or struggle that they want to ask the church to help them in. These are practices which create opportunities for intimacy and for ministering to one another. It is a way of trying to build into our churches the DNA for being like Christ to one another.

I remember when Rebekah and Mary first started coming to one of our churches, Rebekah shared one of the stranger needs I had heard up to that point in my ministry. She said, "I need to stop eating so much Chinese food." We all chuckled a bit. "It's true," Mary chimed in, "all she does is eat take-out and watch Netflix all day!" I did not think much of it at the time, and in fact I forgot about the entire conversation for a time. About 18 months later I was going through the beginning of my divorce. I felt like my whole world was falling apart. When I went to church that afternoon everyone asked me how I was holding up. "I've got Juan holding me accountable for not drinking," I told them. "And Alan has been coming over a lot of evenings just to sit and grieve with me. But it seems like all I did this week was eat take-out and watch Netflix."

I looked across the living room and saw that Rebekah was smiling sadly and nodding her head. "I've been there," she said. It was then that I remembered her need from that church meeting months before. I had not known until later that her marriage was dissolving. I had never put together the connection, but on this day, we had a new bond of intimacy. Rebekah and I shared in our common pain, our common grief, and our common experience of trying to cover ourselves with the meager pleasures of escapism. Although Chinese takeout and Netflix may be on the tame end of the spectrum, they nevertheless are on the spectrum of a common human response to pain and death. Pleasure is a basic way we try to cover our nakedness.

I remember when Juan had to put down his dog, Wilson, after it attacked a man. Wilson was the second largest pit bull I have ever seen (the largest being Wilson's father). Juan took him to the auto-shop with him every day and Wilson would sleep under the tool-bench while the guys worked. Never in my life have I known someone who loved a pet the way Juan loved Wilson. There is no doubt in my mind that, despite the friendship I enjoy with Juan, he was closer to Wilson than to me. I do not feel insulted by that fact. Even now, years later, he brags about that dog the way parents of musical prodigies do of their own offspring. When I found out what had happened, I called, I texted, I went over and knocked on his front door. I spent the whole weekend unable to contact Juan at all. That Monday he asked me to come over. "I can't believe I had to kill my best friend," he told me.

It turns out Juan had stayed high and watched Kung-fu movies on his Playstation from Friday afternoon through the better part of Sunday. He had gone out that morning and bought a miniature Chihuahua who greeted me when I came into the living room. "That's 'little Wilson'," he told me. "I saw him in the petstore and the way he was trying to rip up his blanket, I knew it was Wilson reincarnated." The drinking, the drugs, the movie marathon, the puppy - these were all ways of seeking some pleasure to relieve the pain.

On this particular occasion my being present on the tail-end of Juan's bender actually led to an intimate conversation about his love for Wilson and his own feelings of loneliness. We talked about how unappreciated and uncared for he often feels, and how Wilson had been a frequent source of comfort when Juan felt that way. We talked about how I often feel that way too and that it is friends like Juan and places where I can be vulnerable, like church, that I feel loved in ways that help me deal with the difficult times. The afternoon we hung out was the first time Juan had wanted to be sober for days. I suspect that it was the presence of a loving friend that took away the need to escape, if only momentarily. It is when we find people who can enter into our lives and who are not ashamed of our nakedness that we find the resolve not to use pleasure as a means of covering it.

Cynicism

There are few experiences which boost the ego like smugly dismissing an idealist. "You cannot really still believe that?" the college sophomore says to the freshman. "In time you will come to see that faith is just a crutch," the recently decided atheist tells their Christian friends. "I used to be optimistic like you, but the realities of the work will wear that off of you," the veteran minister says knowingly to the new young preacher. Among the cultured, the educated, and the "experienced" in life, looking down on the dreams of others is frequently a favored pastime. I occasionally refer to this (only slightly joking) as the resurgence of the gnostic heresy: in which strong boundaries of authority, acceptance, and relationship are drawn by those "who really know" what reality is. And this practice is all the more dangerous in our culture, where we have (perhaps intentionally) mistaken cynicism for wisdom.

It is an understandable mix-up. Cynicism looks like wisdom. Cynicism shows that I am not naive, that I know how the world *really* works. It is my license to look down on the hopes of the uninitiated, to criticize the visions of others, and to justify my own apathy and withdrawal from the constant projects of reform which seek to change the status quo. Cynical people are rarely taken advantage of, they are not often disappointed, and they are generally given the respect as ones who have authority - not like the starry-eyed and the optimistic, who will inevitably be crushed under their own ideals as they complete the circle to become the next generation of cynics. If you really want to appear wise, learn cynicism.

The reality, however, is that cynicism is a cover for incredible woundedness. The cynic is often the person who has had their dreams and hopes destroyed, or who so fears failure that they are unwilling to even try to realize those hopes. Cynicism is an armor for protecting ourselves. It is one of the clearest expressions of covering the fear of being hurt. So, the young woman whose parents divorced bitterly after she went to college does not believe in monogamy or marriage. She *knows* those things do not work. The former minister who was abused and uncared for by his first congregation *knows* that there is not any hope to reform the church. The father whose daughter died of Leukemia *knows* that faith is only an emotional placebo. Do not get your hopes up. When the upstart politician who was going to overhaul the political system fails to deliver, those who supported her discover that all politicians are the same. There is no reason to participate in these structures anymore. We now *know* better.

This type of woundedness is tragic and toxic. At its heart, it is only a means of trying to cover our own nakedness. For a culture, however, which

85

lacks models for dealing with disillusionment and pain - and for those who lack the access to other powers - cynicism possess a powerful allure. We may wish we could go back to the hopes and dreams of yesterday, but who wants to remove their armour? It is painful to scrub the calluses off of our hearts, and if the result is that we are only opening ourselves to future pain, then what is the point? It is best not to imagine, not to dream, not to waste our efforts or energies. Better to accept the pointlessness of ideals and learn to guard our hearts against hope. The cynic, more than others, is educated in the knowledge of good and evil.

And, in part, the rejection from "knowing" that exists among the Lost is a form of cynicism. So often my friends have been wounded by religion. For some this is the result of a relationship with a church or Christian friend. For others it is in the disillusionment of seeing a respected spiritual figure brought low through moral failure or abuse of power. In some instances, this cynicism is just a covering of the general feeling of unworthiness they feel, and religion is an easy target in the surrounding culture but hardly the only victim of their deconstructionism. It is for this reason that we must see the rejection from "knowing" as a pastoral rather than a pedagogical need. So often the disillusionment of the Lost covers a deep woundedness and feeling of nakedness. Many feel that they have been measured by Christians and found wanting, and the easiest response is to dismiss the relevancy or the perspective of their perceived antagonists.

Power, pleasure, and cynicism exist in myriad forms both within and outside of our churches. The task of ministers in a post-Christendom culture is to see these for what they are: coverings of our nakedness and shame. It is only when we are able to clearly see and identify with these experiences of woundedness and fear that we can respond appropriately - as ones who also feel vulnerable and experience Sin but who have discovered a better model of responding to our humanity in Jesus. It is only in coming alongside others and bonding over what it is like to be human that we can testify to the fact that we know one who is "like God."

Section III

What is Jesus Like?

Chapter 7

Christ's Place in the Order of Things

Do nothing from selfish ambition or conceit, but in humility regard others as better than yourselves. Let each of you look not to your own interests, but to the interests of others. Let the same mind be in you that was in Christ Jesus, who, though he was in the very nature of God, did not regard equality with God as something to be exploited, but emptied himself, taking the form of a slave, being born in human likeness. And being found in human form, he humbled himself and became obedient to the point of death—even death on a cross. Therefore God also highly exalted him and gave him the name that is above every name, so that at the name of Jesus every knee should bend, in heaven and on earth and under the earth, and every tongue should confess that Jesus Christ is Lord, to the glory of God the Father
-Philippians 2:3-11

I recall going to Vacation Bible School at the Alameda Church of Christ when I was a young child in Norman, Oklahoma. The song leader would stand on the stage and lead us in familiar songs to which were often added exaggerated motions or faux sign-language, and among these songs "Lord, I Lift Your Name On High" stands out in my memory. The chorus goes as follows: "He came from Heaven to Earth to show the way. From the

Earth to the Cross, my debt to pay. From the Cross to the Grave, from the Grave to the Sky: Lord I lift your name on high." Reflecting on these lyrics as an adult, I have, on the one hand, some concerns and objections about the wisdom of teaching children that Jesus lives in the sky (of more positive interest to me is the song's sense of what "name" means theologically, but more on that later). However, I also see in this worship song an act similar to what I think Paul is doing in his letter to the church in Philippi. In both hymns we find a particular articulation of the mythic arc worked out in the person of Jesus of Nazareth:

In some way, the church claims, the identity of Christ originates in the being of God. And this divine being found itself in the human person of Jesus - a man who lived, loved, taught, and died within our own world and history. For those of us who are followers of Jesus, we believe that God resurrected him from death and that something in this arc reveals a deep Truth about the nature of God and the purpose of human life and community. And we mythologize this narrative in song and in the many symbols and rituals of faith: in eucharist, baptism, the cross that hangs from a necklace, the nativity scene we set out every winter, and so on. In our monastic community in Texas the older initiates would wash the feet of the new initiates at our annual induction. We did this because in some way it seemed to embody and express something profound about what we had seen revealed in Jesus that was easier to articulate in action than words alone.

This narrative of self-emptying and embracing death, along with the life of imitation which emerges from it - what we will call discipleship - are what I will henceforth refer to as the Christ myth.[16] It is the theological reality that we seek to convey when we speak of "the good news," the story of the cross, or simply invoke the name: Jesus. And as we are attempting to speak about the implications of a life which, evidently, could not be captured by all the books in the world (John 21:25), I will, here, constrain myself to a

---

[16] I would argue that the Christ myth is one that is both historically true but seeks to gesture towards profound truths with greater consequence to the nature of reality than simply their factual accuracy as past events.

few observations about the Christ myth and the life and teachings of Jesus which I think are significant for helping us establish a theology of what Jesus is like. But first a word on method.

In the following section I am not going to make any real effort to differentiate between the human person of Jesus and the Christ. I will use these terms somewhat interchangeably in the following chapters with little distinction except to point out that Jesus was a Jewish laborer and prophet who lived an itinerant life in Palestine in the first century of the common era; Christ is a title bestowed upon him (the Hellenization of the Hebrew title "Messiah"): it is the claim that he is God's anointed one.

Looking at the Christ myth, as it is condensed in Paul's words at the beginning of this chapter, there are three principles I would like to draw out and which I think are in harmony with the Evangelists' various accounts of Jesus, the Messiah. First, Jesus was like us. Another way to say this is that, whatever else he was, Jesus was a human being. And if this is the case then we might expect what we said of what it is like to be human to be true of Jesus: Jesus was a maker and shaper of reality, Jesus was known and came to be understood through the relationships he maintained - i.e. Jesus knew both intimacy and loneliness - and Jesus knew and shared in our nakedness. I plan to examine the significance of this in the following chapters, as I think it important to spend some time immersed in this most fundamental claim if we are to find our way forward in creating a reorienting theology.

The second observation I would make is that Jesus' death was a product of his obedience. While many sound arguments have been set out, historically, about the cross being an act of obedience to God's ultimate plan of salvation, I would like here to reflect on it in a particular way: Jesus' death - and that on a cross, no less - is a product of his being intolerable to the order of things. In this sense it was "because of Sin" that he died, but not simply in substitution for our sins. For reasons we will explore, death was the inevitable consequence for the Christ's obedience to his own nature.

And, as I hope we will see, this was not in the same way that death is the end for all humans.

In some way particular to his own person, the death of Jesus is one which contained within it a political and social drama that tore the veil of the temple and exposes so many of the idols we create. While I have frequently been critical of how often we reduce the gospel to solely the death of Jesus and truncate the good news to substitutionary atonement, I do think that we find in the cross a convergence of seeming paradoxes about Jesus outside of which it is impossible to understand the nature of the Christ, and subsequently of the God whose anointed one he is. On the crossed beams upon which he was executed by the powers that be, we witness a tension of profound Truths about the nature of Jesus, the Christ, and of God.

Finally, in this section, we will explore the way in which, through his resurrection, Jesus was vindicated. In overturning violence and death as the ultimate powers at our disposal, God has made a statement about who Jesus is as a human being as well as who he is in being God's own representative. We find in the resurrection an affirmation of the Christ as the model of a whole human person, but we find God's rejection of our claims as to the supremacy of our own theologies as well. When Jesus sought to reveal to us "what God is like," we tried him for blasphemy. When Jesus revealed the falseness of our idolatrous games and refused to serve any Kingdom without a character like God's, we sought to cover over this breach of the system, thinking it better for this man to die than for the whole of what we had built to perish and descend into chaos (John 11:47-49).

As we shall discuss, when a system cannot discredit or pervert that which unmasks its false authority, death is the final power at its disposal. The resurrection of Jesus vindicates him as the one who truly speaks on behalf of God. In living fully into his identity, Jesus was given a new name that is above all names, *Lord*. His new life initiates the reordering of things and the restoration of God's intended relationship with all of creation: in reflecting on what Jesus - the anointed and resurrected one of God - is like we come to answer the question of what it could be like to be human because we begin to see more fully what God, whose image we bear, is like.

Chapter 8

The Nature of Jesus as Creator and Shaper

"You have heard it said...but I tell you." If I had to encapsulate the thesis of Jesus' work into one phrase, this is a serious contender. I tell you: love your enemies, don't be afraid, the greatest among you is the least, whatever you do for the least of these you do for me, take up your cross and follow me. Jesus embraced his human capacity as one in the creative image of God to directly engage the powers that be. He ate with "sinners," he broke the Sabbath law, he redefined words like "family" and "Kingdom," he turned purity codes on their head by touching diseased people. He saw through the dehumanizing rules of the games played around him - our slavery to the systems we had created - and he responded with a deep understanding and solidarity. "I know what you have heard the High Priest say, what you heard Caesar say, what you have heard said by culture and tradition, and even what you have said about yourselves. But let me tell you something different." In this sense, by obeying his own nature, Jesus entered into an inevitable conflict with Sin in its institutional manifestations.

Let us take a brief but much discussed example that many of our churches have been working through over the last few years. "You have heard it said, 'Eye for eye and tooth for tooth,' but I tell you do not resist an evil person. If someone strikes you on the right cheek, turn to him the other also. And if someone sues you for your coat, give them your cloak as well. If someone forces you to go one mile with them, go with them two. Give to the one who asks and do not turn away from the one who seeks to borrow from you" (Matt. 5:38-42). My experience is that, upon a first reading, no one likes this passage. Particularly in the Bronx, where *Lex Talionis* is one of the few moral imperatives, Jesus, here, seems insane.[17] I have had Juan and Mary tell me as much in conflict, and can say that this was not much better received by our church in the East Village, initially. "Does Jesus want us to be victims? Are we supposed to just let people walk all over us?," I have been asked. I partially suspect that we read victimhood into so many of Jesus' teachings because we have told the gospel as if that is what Jesus is like: a victim who, out of love, could not defend himself. But when we dig deeper into the dynamics of what is being described in this passage, things are not exactly as they may appear.

In each of the scenarios posed by Jesus in these verses we have an interaction between two people in which one is being dominated by the other. While vague, we can point out a few points which are definite: the first is some sort of interpersonal grievance, the second is legal (most likely to do with a debt), and the third is political - as "forcing someone to go a mile" is certainly a reference to the common practice of Roman soldiers demanding dominated subjects of the Empire carry their packs while on marching routes. And in each scenario, we may presume, the dominated person has been subjected to the normal limit of oppression: to be struck on the face is to be insulted, perhaps backhanded, as an inferior; the legal limit of the law permitted the taking of the inner garment in court by the party owed but not the outer garment;[18] and a Roman soldier was legally forbidden to force conscripted laborers beyond a single mile.[19]

So, what we have prescribed, here, is not in the context of simple relational conflict. It is oppression. In that light the responses are more

---

[17] *Lex Talionis* is a law of equivalent injury such as the one depicted in Exodus 21:23-25. For more see Robert Alter, *The Five Books of Moses* (W.W. Norton & Company: New York, NY, 2004), 440.

[18] See Deuteronomy 24:10-13

[19] For more see Walter Wink, *Jesus and Nonviolence: A Third Way* (Fortress Press: Minneapolis, MN, 2003), 9-28.

subversive than they first seem. "If someone strikes you on the right cheek, turn to him the other also." I am reminded of a scene in the movie Fight Club[20] where the angry mobster landlord, Lou, has his henchman beat Brad Pitt's character in front of his men to teach him a lesson. After each round of punches Pitt continues to say, "Still not getting it Lou," as he is more and more grossly abused. Finally disturbed and disgusted the henchman runs out of the basement with Pitt's character yelling, "Come back Lou, we really like it here!" Gratuitous though this scene may be, it is of a similar kind of resistance that I think we find in our passage in Matthew 5. I have been backhanded before; it is humiliating. And the normal response would be either to submit to humiliation or to hit back. But imagine what sort of response it would evoke to turn your face and say, "Better get this side too." Now the script has been interrupted. The would-be victim has refused to be humiliated and in doing so recalibrated the dynamic. Rather than "resist an evil person" the cruelty is allowed to play out until it reveals itself for what it truly is, and in this revelation its power is lost.

"If someone sues you and takes your coat, give him your cloak as well." The second scenario reminds me of one of the great scenes in *Les Miserables*. Parolee Jean ValJean has stolen from the monastery which took him in and has been apprehended by the police. As he is a recently released felon, he is now going to be placed back into prison, most likely for life. But when confronted with the thief, the Bishop simply says (and I'm paraphrasing), "I gave him those things. And, sir, you forgot the best pieces." He then proceeds to give him the silver candlesticks. The mercy in this scene is touching, and clearly Hugo knew something about what Jesus was like to depict such a stirring account of the grace and hospitality practiced among monks. But in the scenario in Matthew 5 the power dynamics are even more unfairly set. A debtor is being sued and their only asset is the very shirt on their back. And what does Jesus tell this victim of the courts? Essentially,

---

[20] *Fight Club*. Directed by David Fincher. Performed by Brad PItt and Edward Norton. United States: 20th Century Fox, 1999.

"strip naked and give it all to your accuser." I can only imagine the disorder this would bring into the proceedings. Now, rather than being humiliated by the verdict, the injustice of the entire trial has been exposed. The notion that it might be fair to take from the poor everything up to their next to last article of clothing in order to make sure they repay a debt has been shown for what it is: mock justice. Again, we find that what we thought was transpiring is not actually what is being asked of the disciples. Refusal to resist evil on its own terms has undone it without the victim validating the proceedings by participating as expected. Jesus is more creative and subversive than it may initially have appeared.

Finally, carrying a Roman soldier's pack. Because of the generation I was born into, many of my friends, classmates, and coworkers over the years are now veterans of the War(s) in the Middle East. In speaking with those who have wished to speak about their service, one of the details that has stood out to me over the years has been the difficulty many had in relating to the local population. A diverse range of experiences and emotions accompanied their tenure as an occupying force, but particularly difficult for many of them to parse were the occasions when they received kindness from strangers. While my veteran friends had positive interactions - they encountered grateful people, in some cases they saved lives or livelihoods of locals - the experiences of strangers approaching or helping them when unprovoked warranted suspicion more often than a sense of appreciation. Why is this person helping me? Is this a trap? These are the questions my friends have related to me as feeling on numerous occasions, and they are the natural response of one who anticipates resistance in the face of their authority. For a people, like the original hearers of the gospel, who were resentfully under occupation by an imperial oppressor, to go out of one's way to help a foreign military presence raises all sorts of questions about where dignity and authority are truly derived.

So, we have an example of Jesus' teaching, but what does this teach about what he was *like*? Near the end of the gospels, we see the way in which

Jesus worked out this same sense of creativity and subversion in his own life and ministry. After a series of false and contradictory witnesses give testimony at his trial before the Sanhedrin, Jesus is taken before Pilate, the Roman prefect of Judea. "Pilate asked him, 'Are you the King of the Jews?' He answered him, 'You say so.' Then the chief priests accused him of many things. Pilate asked him again, "Have you no answer? See how many charges they bring against you?' But Jesus made no further reply, so that Pilate was amazed" (Mark 15:2-5). It is clear as the story proceeds that Pilate does not find the evidence against Jesus convincing. It is also clear that the court of priests and the accusing crowd know this is a sham. So why does Jesus keep silent? Why does he refuse to defend himself in this kangaroo court? My suspicion is that the most damning response to this injustice is to not dignify it with a defense. Jesus here is a victim, but he is not powerless or a doormat. The silence of Jesus hangs over the whole charade of his trial, challenging us to see - if we will - that it is all just a cruel and stupid fiction. The principalities can accuse, and they can kill. They have that *power*. But they have no authority over the Christ.

Claiming the Game

In the last section, we discussed the way in which - by nature of being human- we create systems and powers which take on our own fallenness. But through Jesus' own life and ministry we are propositioned with a question: what if a large enough group of people agreed to change the way the game is played? What if a cohort within the game, within the dominion of the powers, decided to take the very language and rules of the system and to subvert them from within? What would happen then? I am reminded of a scene from the 1982 movie Gandhi. Speaking of the British colonial powers, Ben Kingsley's character says, "They may torture my body, break my bones, even kill me. Then they will have my dead body, but not my obedience."[21] I am also reminded of a game of Settlers of Catan which some of the members of my former monastic community were playing some years ago. If you do not know Catan, it is a board game in which players participate in a small bartering economy based on cards won through the rolling of various combinations of dice. The purpose of the game is to acquire the necessary resources to build your own society, with various achievements in building earning points for the player. The first player to achieve a certain number of points wins.

I have played many games of Catan. I highly recommend it to you. But almost every time I play it evolves in the same fashion: when one player begins to approach the number of points necessary to win, the other players begin to try to prevent them from pulling ahead. There is nowhere in the rules where this is instructed. It is simply the competitive nature of most players that, despite gladly trading and cooperating with one another at the beginning, when the game nears the end, they turn against the person most likely to win. People stop trading with her, people intentionally try to undermine her building projects, people might steal from her and feel justified. It is, again, a microcosm of human institutions. It is the principalities and powers of our nature played out on a very small and relatively harmless scale.

On this particular occasion, however, one of the brothers from the community decided - just to make things interesting - to "play like Jesus." He very faithfully gave to the ones who asked and did not turn away from anyone who wished to borrow from him. And, like Jesus warned, he was taken advantage of and abused within the available limits of the game. But as the game progressed something interesting began to take place: those to whom he had lent felt more generous both with him and with one another. They had not had to work for all of their resources; Kyle (the Christlike player) would obviously help them if they made a bad trade. Why not be

---

[21] *Gandhi*, Directed by Richard Attenborough. Performed by Sir Ben Kingsley. United States: Columbia Pictures, 1982.

more open-handed with their cards? So they were. Then even those players who had decided to spite Kyle and score an easy victory were shamed into changing the game. What did their victory mean if everyone else was going to achieve the same number of points without competing against one another? By refusing to play the game "the right way" Kyle ended up subverting the entire thing. This is a principle I like to call **claiming the game,** and I think it is the mentality that Jesus models for us if we wish to live as humans in a sane world.

The difficulty of claiming the game, however, is that to do so we must admit that it is *only* a game. We must deliberately will away our own blindness and forfeit the security or advantages we have received from playing. In doing this we take a great risk. We will almost inevitably be taken advantage of. Further, if we stop playing, we will almost certainly lose the game. At first this may not sound like a problem: why would someone care about losing a game they are not trying to win? But this overlooks the great psychological force the powers have. Who has not wanted to pull the curtain back closed and pretend that the Wizard of Oz still exists; to enter back into the fantasy that we have not just been working for "the man" who is only pulling levers and shouting into a machine? To forfeit our games of status, security, and power is to forfeit the whole world, nearly.

If we are the only ones who stop playing, we fear we will inevitably be classified as madmen, radicals, anarchists, or fools. Or we may not be taken seriously and simply be labeled "sore losers." If we stop playing as a group, it is likely that we will still be named these things; we will just have company. The powers are so pervasive that it is nearly impossible for an individual to stop playing unless that person totally retreats from society. This is why we cannot fully claim the game merely as individuals. We must do it in community. We must create alternative zones from which to invert the principalities and powers from within, but within a space in which we know we are loved, we can be vulnerable, and we are free to creatively imagine alternatives to the normative outcome of playing along with the powers that be. And we must have a deep faith that, at the end of the day, it is a better outcome to lose through "playing like Jesus" than to win by the rules of a game based on overreaching and domination. Jesus, himself, described this as making a choice against "gaining the whole world and losing your soul" (Mk 8:36).

Playing the Kingdom of God

When I look at the various configurations of human society and the diverse games we play, I can think of no groups of people who have done a better job of claiming the game than those which have been founded upon Jesus' teachings about community. This should probably not surprise us as Jesus and his disciples were constantly in trouble for claiming the game, or (as it was called in their day) not keeping Sabbath, not observing the traditions of the elders, taking the lowest place, and eating with sinners. The church in the book of Acts, the monastic communities of the desert fathers, the anabaptist communities on the edge of urban societies, the urban churches who have embraced and supported immigrant communities, the Christian celibates and young marrieds who have moved into the housing projects of "the hood" and become, not gentrifiers, but the neighbors and friends of "the poor" - these seem to me to be among the clearest pictures I have seen of people claiming the game in our world. These are the communities which I have witnessed best unmask the principalities and powers of their day and invert the competitiveness and divisiveness of created systems with a sort of playful anarchy. They have done so in the name of an alternative game of imagination - a counter reality - which scripture calls "The Kingdom of God."

I would like to share two stories from the desert fathers which I think illustrate this principle well. In Scetis one of the brothers was once found guilty of a severe sin. The monks were assembled and sent a message to Abba Moses telling him to come. But he would not come. Then the presbyter sent for Moses again saying, "Come, for the gathering of the monks is waiting for you." Moses got up and went, but first he took an old basket, filled it with sand, and placed it on his back. When the monks went up to meet him, they saw the sand pouring from the basket and they asked, "Abba, what does this mean?" He said, "My sins run out behind me and I do not see them, and I have come here today to judge another." They listened to him and said nothing more to the brother who had sinned but forgave him.[22]

On another occasion Arsenius was speaking with an old Egyptian monk, he was asking advice about dealing with temptation. Another monk who saw this said, "Arsenius, how is it that you, who are so well educated in Greek and Latin, are asking that ignorant peasant about temptations?" Arsenius answered him, "I have a lot of worldly knowledge of Greek and of Latin, but I have not yet been able to learn the alphabet of this peasant."[23] The abbas knew that worldly authority and academic accreditation are just games. There is no reason to let these institutions dictate how we treat one another in the Kingdom of God. In imitation of Jesus, they found the creative capacity to look through the game and see what was necessary for the flourishing of human relationship.

The gamification of church is something I try to embrace in the spiritual formation of our communities. A religious body is full of rules, offices, titles, liturgies, and traditions, all of which are elements of the games particular to a denomination or heritage. And I am not saying these are bad things, but I am saying they are a part of our human propensity to institutionalize. I want to help my friends realize how free they are to ask questions about the nature of religious things and to think critically about the structures and practices which their acquaintanceship with Christendom culture has led they assume *must* be a part of faith.

One instance of dealing with this that stands out in my memory is the first night I hung out with Juan's friends from work. We had all gone out to see a new distillery which was being built in the South Bronx, then we

---

[22] *The Desert Fathers: Sayings of the Early Christian Monks,* translated by Benedicta Ward (Penguin Books: London, England, 2003), 85.
[23] *The Desert Fathers,* Ward, 149.

went out for tacos, and finally came back to our regular bar to have a pint and call it a night. As the evening settled into that relaxed lower gear that sometimes accompanies groups moving to their final activity together, Juan's friends began to ask me more about the church-planting I do and what it is like. I felt honored by the opportunity to share stories from the gospels and about different ways I had seen God work in the lives of members of our gatherings but was not surprised by this crew's initial reaction. "You'll never see me in a church," one man said. Everyone around the table laughed and nodded their heads in agreement.

I laughed, too, and I said to him. "At the churches we start, everybody sits around a table, shares a meal, and we talk about who Jesus is and how what he taught affects the way we live. How is that any different from what we're doing right now? The only difference I can see between the churches I go to and what we're doing now is the label." And then I watched the lightbulb start to turn on for people around the table. "So, you're telling me," the man replied, "that if we kept showing up and having conversations like this, we could be a church?" I told him I did not see any reason why that would not be the case. Who is going to keep that from being church? "Isn't that what Jesus and his disciples are doing in all the stories we've been talking about tonight?" I asked him. He thought for a minute and then responded, "I could go to a church like this."

Part of claiming the game is to try to undermine those categories and unquestioned assumptions which "box in" or "box out" the ministry of Kingdom. I was having a conversation with a leader who was part of Mary and Rebekah's house church network and whom I had been discipling for about 18 months and he told me he was going to go a local congregation to be ordained by the bishop there. I was surprised and I asked him how he had reached that decision. He explained that he had been hanging out with some members from this congregation and they had told him he needed to be ordained to lead the church he was a part of. He had felt the lack of ordination in his ministry ever since; so much so that he, on their advice, was beginning to lay aside various leadership roles he had already been doing in order to await the approval of this other congregation's leadership. "Well," I told him, "I am not going to stop you from going, but you started that church and have been leading it ever since your baptism. I'm curious what it is they are going to give you that will add to that. Help me understand: don't you disciple others with the authority you receive from having God's spirit? Is there something ordination is going to give you which will give you more authority or competence?"

He said he would think about the question and he later decided not to pursue ordination. "I guess," he said, "that what gives them the authority to ordain me would be the same spirit which God has already given me to minister." To my mind this is an example of a new disciple claiming the game. This is not to suggest that ordination is bad or should be done away with. In this instance, however, the rules of the game were beginning to choke out ministry - the very end to which those rules are designed to serve.

On another occasion I was catching up with my friend KJ, as we had not spoken in a month or so. She began to tell me about how difficult her previous week had been. One of her good friends and fellow musicians had relapsed into an addiction and she had sat on the phone with him for several hours while he came down from a high. "I know that isn't a very spiritual thing," she told me, "but I just couldn't help but feel like Christ was present on the phone with us." I asked her what she meant that this call had not been a spiritual thing. She paused and considered the question before responding, "I guess anything in relationship is open to being spiritual." She laughed. "Why would we limit the things God is a part of to a certain category of only 'spiritual things?'" I told her I thought that was a very good question, and I smiled because I got to see the Kingdom being played out.

Thinking about these things, I am reminded of a story my family likes to retell about my great-grandfather. He had been a preacher in small churches of Christ in West Texas, and in his older years was approached by someone who asked him, "Clarence, can a woman preach?" To speak about it in our terms, this is an inquiry trying to establish the *right* way to play church. "Well," my great-grandfather responded after a moment, "some of them can, and some of them can't." This story is an enduring example to me of someone who understands the difference between playing in the Kingdom and playing another game. It seems to me that maintaining such discernment takes a lot of creativity and more than a little humility.

Gaming as Formation

One of my favorite things to do in our communities is to create small playful ways to help us begin to practice the values of the Kingdom. Playfulness is an underappreciated aspect of our humanity, especially in regard to the spiritual disciplines. I want to try to turn our creative capacity into a tool which helps develop holy habits and Christlike character. I want to help people learn to play Kingdom by redeeming their imaginations. A simple way we did this in our Texas monastic community - which I have occasionally adopted in church groups - is that when we met together for a meal, no one is allowed to serve themselves and no one is allowed to ask for anything. It is a seemingly silly game, but it creates a culture of service and attention. I can nearly promise that no sermon about "looking out for the needs of and serving one another" is as effective as this simple game.

There is another exercise I do when church groups are too large and people begin to compete with one another for attention. I tell everyone to break off for the discussion of scripture into groups of three or four and, when we come back, no one is allowed to share any insights which they had. Everyone who speaks can only speak on behalf of someone else in their group. It is a bit childish, but this game can change the entire culture of a meeting. People begin to learn to listen and to pay attention to one another rather than simply waiting for their turn to speak. People are forced into some humility when the insight they were so proud of does not get brought back up in the big group. This is a small game which begins to help churches play out the values of Kingdom and the character of Jesus.

When one of my friends has a hard time learning to pray, I sometimes counsel them to pick a noise, like the sound of their phone or the honking of a car horn. I tell them that every time they hear that sound, they should stop what they are doing for 10 seconds, smile, and say "Thank you, God, for this moment." This game begins to generate a consistent awareness of God's presence and availability. Or when people have trouble learning when to give to the poor I've often counseled them to have a special pocket in their coat or purse and to put a few dollars in that pocket every time they get back change after making a purchase (NYC is still a place that operates on hard cash). New York is a city with a never-ending stream of need which can easily overwhelm anyone's capacity to give, so it can be difficult to know when and in what way to respond. Whenever someone comes and asks for money, I suggest, just give them whatever is in that pocket. If nothing is there, just say that you are sorry but you do not have anything to give them.

These little games, though seemingly insignificant, begin to slowly transform the imagination and the habits of people seeking to imitate Jesus. These are small steps toward redeeming the creative capacity which is so fundamental to our humanity. Creating practices like these in a community of new disciples works to develop a culture of experimentation and playfulness, which I find to be so integral to forming healthy Christian leaders who are not driven by the fear of failure. It empowers new and pre-believers to examine the elements of their lives which are seemingly so "unspiritual." Trying to imagine and practice the Kingdom they find a vast array of resources already in their possession which only need to be reused or recycled in order to bring them closer to the will of God.

These "small games" begin to constitute the ministry of the church and to become powerful tools against the principalities and powers which oppose Kingdom and constrain the lives of people. They are very approachable ways for the number of the Lost who belong to our communities but have not yet decided who Jesus is to begin putting into practice the things which he would ask them to do. And I would argue that it is only through the practice of following Jesus that any of us come to discover who he is. It is in the imitation of the Christ that we begin to discern what he is like.

I would challenge you to find your own means of creating and shaping community in a way that calls people deeper into the playful imitation of Christ, and to invest the time and the energy to create a culture of experimentation and gamification in the spiritual formation of the Lost. But I would caution against making these practices too rigid. It is my suspicion that Torah - although it is always a discipline - becomes a burden only after it ceases to be a joy, and that when we replace the playfulness and creative subversion of Kingdom games with legalism then we have begun to create another power under which we must serve.

Chapter 9

The Nature of Jesus in Relationship

After my wife left, I took a 30 day sabbatical to a hermitage in South Texas. I was broken beyond anything I had imagined, and I was afraid my ongoing presence in NYC would be toxic to the ministry I had worked to form up to that point. The nakedness in me had been forcibly put on full display and I wanted to reach for anything at hand to cover it. My insecurity and pain were calling out to take hold of everyone around me and use them to fill the void in my own heart, so the best solution I could devise was to go away from people for a time and be in solitude with God. I spent a month alone and unspeaking in a small cell provided by the religious order who operated the hermitage, and I dwelt in that time in the presence of the only one who has the power to heal and to restore life.

I especially recall one afternoon several weeks into my sabbatical when I was praying in my cell where a large ivory colored crucifix hung on the wall. As I was raised Protestant it is always somewhat jarring to see that, in Catholic imagery, Jesus typically remains on the cross. And in attending to this picture I recognized a solidarity with Christ that I had not before: "I, too, am alone," it seemed to say to me. "I, also, know what it feels like to be betrayed and abandoned. I understand..." And I wept for the first time in that season from gratitude instead of shame. This is one of many profound ways that Jesus is like us.

Public and Private Jesus

I am not certain that you're supposed to have a favorite gospel, but mine is Mark. It is short and action packed (everything seems to happen "immediately" after the last thing), which suits my attention span, and I am fascinated by how inscrutable Jesus is in comparison with the portraits of him in the other gospels. His emotional life, as depicted in Mark, is of a bizarre range. In my recent readings of the book, I made an attempt to note all the "feeling" words I could find associated with Jesus: I found that he was "stern," "angry," "indignant," "distressed," "aggrieved," he does a great deal of rebuking (which is a bit ambiguous as to the exact emotional tenor, but hardly to be desired). Twice he "sighs" before doing a miracle (*ibid.*), a couple of times he is "astounded by [a group's] lack of faith," and he is constantly warning people not to tell anyone about him. On the positive side, he loved the rich young ruler when he sees him and twice he has compassion on a crowd - once because they are like sheep without a shepherd, and another time because they haven't eaten in days.

Granted, by limiting the reading to explicit "feelings" I am not accounting for some of the more emotionally moving depictions of the Markan Jesus - such as his interaction with the woman suffering from hemorrhages in chapter 5 - but this is a Jesus whose emotional life differs from what one might expect if they were to sit in on the typical Christian worship service. Jesus does not seem always peaceful and warm. He is often brusque and seems at odds with those around him. He does not seem to seek after worship and praise. In fact, one is left at the end of the gospel wondering how much Jesus desires to be the center of attention: besides his liberal use of the gag-rule for miracle recipients, in four of the accounts of him healing people he takes them away from any onlookers before getting to work. And at least seven separate times Mark recounts him dismissing a crowd out of a desire to be alone. Mark's Jesus is constantly going away to lonely places just when it seems like his preaching has conjured an audience. Why all the feelings of distress? Why the reticence to embrace attention and adoration? I would argue that the answer lies in Jesus' understanding of how relationships play into human identity.

For every crowd that forms around him, if we look closely, we will find a collection of competing identities with respect to who Jesus is and what it means for him to be the Messiah. When he enters a town, all the sick gather in such great numbers that there is no room to even stand much less engage them on an individual level. But Jesus knows the Christ is more than a Great Physician. When Jesus goes out into the desert, a veritable army of 5,000 men follows him out, and a charismatic leader who can feed the masses from virtually nothing and raise the dead is an appealing figure for a people looking to reclaim their homeland. But that isn't the kind of king the Christ has come to be. When his family sees him working, they try to bring him home for fear that he's gone mad. When he does go home the whole town grumbles at his teaching, "Isn't this the carpenter, Mary's son? When did he get so high and mighty?" Even among his own disciples, only one out of twelve knows the answer to a question any Sunday School child couldn't get wrong, "You are the Messiah" (Mk 8:29). But a few minutes later that one is being called "Satan," because he rebuked the Christ for talking about dying on a cross.

Jesus knows, it seems, that if we are not careful to retreat to lonely places and pray, that the image of ourselves others try to mirror to us may call us away from the identity God has given us. He is so centered in what it means to be *truly* God's anointed one, that in order to love others he must constantly step away from the crowds, from the adoration, from the seeming success of his ministry; because the crowd that sings "Hosanna to the King" when the week begins is the same that chants "Crucify him!" at the end of the week. It is only through a discipline and practice in solitude with God that Jesus maintains his identity, from which his capacity to love and to give of himself to others is drawn.

Jesus does not fall into the temptation that so many of us do: to use the people around him to create for himself a sense of identity, meaning, and purpose. He goes a step further, however, and does what I would consider an equally difficult thing for one in a life of ministry. The Christ refuses to be used by those around him to act as someone or something to them that he is not. He gives freely of himself, but his love for others prevents him from diverging from his nature in order to please or serve them. It is this deeply rooted sense of identity in God that I think allows for Jesus' sinlessness. It is also the obedience to this identity that will cause him to disappoint and offend almost everyone around him. In becoming obedient to his nature, Jesus becomes a danger to all competing definitions of *Christ*. It is this disillusionment with who God has chosen as anointed - the failure of Jesus to be the Christ we want or imagine - which ultimately lead to the betrayal, abandonment, and death of the Messiah.

A "Relatable" Figure

I don't feel the way about America's political heroes that I used to. Growing up in public schools around Oklahoma and Texas, we were made to memorize parts of the Declaration of Independence and the Gettysburg Address, we read the Bill of Rights, the Federalist Papers, and listened to speeches by Teddy and Franklin Roosevelt. And we learned about Martin Luther King and Malcolm X. We studied the deeds of Civil War generals. But in my adult life I have read biographies of almost all the people behind these "great" ideas and deeds. And in seeing their lives beyond their words and institutional achievements my respect and beliefs about them have shifted. My esteem for some has risen and for others has been lost; my point here being that no figure can be very much understood without insight into who they are as a person in relationship with others. As we saw in Genesis, it is not good for us to be alone, and so often our ability to idolize our fellow humans is predicated on our willfully ignoring how they related to and were perceived by those around them. I think it is for this reason that we have, in the gospels, so many stories of Jesus interacting with other people. The Evangelists could easily have given us simply a collection of sayings, but they chose instead to tell us stories from the day to day interactions of the Christ as he encountered others. I don't mean to suggest by this that the four gospels fall into the genre that we would think of as biography, but it does strike me that - if the authors of Scripture were concerned with capturing the humanity of Jesus - they were wise to show us a person who is in relationship.

Learning in Community

At the outset of all our church plants, we have begun with one of the gospels. More often than not, I have had groups begin reading scripture in the Sermon on the Mount. In addition to being the text around which my former monastic community built our rule of life, I think Matthew 5-7 is the clearest manifesto of a life built around the imitation of Christ. If there was a rule book on how to play Kingdom, these teachings would be at the center of it. And when our church groups are first forming, the way we engage Scripture is built around a common set of questions. We begin by discussing things we are thankful for since our last meeting, then we ask what needs and struggles each of us have at the moment and how we might help one another meet those needs. As I mentioned previously, these initial questions become the foundation around which praise and one another ministry are built as the group begins to develop in faith. Following these we read scripture and ask four questions: "What does this teach us about who God is?," "What does this teach us about life?," "How will we put this into practice this week?," and "Who will we share this with?" Our hope is that in structuring these gatherings as an inductive and self-correcting dialogue with Scripture as the authority at its center, we create churches that are not only highly reproducible by everyday disciples, but which also are communities of praxis for those seeking to follow Jesus in order to determine whether or not they believe he is Christ and Lord.

Our communities operate this way because we are attempting to replicate something we see in the pedagogy of Jesus: a respect for

113

relationships and communal discernment. Unlike so many philosophies of teaching employed in our world, Jesus' is one in which we - as fellow human beings - are invited to be discoverers and participants. For every direct teaching like the Sermon on the Mount, there are parables and object lessons that we are invited to hear, if we have the ears to. For every new command, there is an interaction around a table that Jesus is calling us to interpret and respond to for ourselves. Jesus may frequently make an "I am" statement - "the Bread of Life," "the Good Shepherd," etc - but he also draws us into the conversation asking, "Who do you say that I am?" It is this collaborative and inductive style of evangelism and formation that we seek to emulate in our disciple-making work. We do this because we see modeled in Jesus a way of teaching that embraces the relationships formed in community as the locus for discerning and working out the implications of the good news about God's Kingdom. This is, in part, what we referred to in a previous chapter as **"discovery"** and **"process orientation."**

And when this sort of culture is utilized in the disciple-making process, it not only shapes the content and style of our teaching to closer resemble what we see in Scripture - one with the relational nature of human beings as central to our identities - it also facilitates a way of being church that fosters and empowers the priesthood of all believers. So when KJ goes on tour with her band, she doesn't need years of seminary training or a set of lesson plans to gather everyone around Scripture and ask questions. And she doesn't have to be intimidated about not having all the answers to everyone's inquiries because she is not expected to be the center of authority and knowledge. She is able to facilitate the discovery and mutual seeking of her friends and do so in a way that respects their prior knowledge and experiences as partners in a dialogue. And I often will walk into Juan's auto-shop and hear him telling a customer one of the parables that I told him a few days before, and he is asking them, "What do you think this story is supposed to teach about how to live?" And this is not a bait and switch question on a tract pushing them toward conversion, it is a genuine example of people connecting around a story and seeking together to discover answers.

So, as we seek to emulate the life of Jesus, we do so not as individuals but in community. And what we see in Jesus' own person is a balance of intimacy and loneliness. He often withdraws so that he can then engage. He gives and reveals of himself, but then he must go away or move on to the next town. And in the communities he forms, the very nature of the relationships works to facilitate the communal discernment of how to live in Kingdom together. These gatherings must be made up of individuals who are deeply grounded in solitude, who know their own calling and identity before God, but who come together ready to discover and learn from one another. This is a body formed by Christ, it is a body which seeks to imitate Christ. This way of - while grounded in a contemplative attention to God - seeking after and imagining together an alternative to the order of things is what we call, "Church." It is how we seek to form communities who are *like* Jesus in our world.

Chapter 10

The Nature of Jesus as *Lord*

A man planted a vineyard, put a fence around it, dug a pit for the wine press, and built a watchtower; then he leased it to tenants and went to another country. When the season came, he sent a slave to the tenants to collect from them his share of the produce of the vineyard. But they seized him and beat him, and sent him away empty handed. And again he sent another slave to them, this one they beat over the head and insulted. Then he sent another, and that one they killed. And so it was with many others; some they beat, and others they killed. He had still one other, a beloved son. Finally he sent him to them, saying, 'They will respect my son.' But those tenants said to one another, 'This is the heir; come, let us kill him and the inheritance will be ours.' So they seized him, killed him, and threw him out of the vineyard.
-Mark 12:1-8

    I inherited from my mother a love of wordplay. This has led to a life of causing groans at dinner parties and of appreciating Scripture. If you are not already aware, the biblical library is full of wordplay. The Hebrew writers especially are fond of homophones and witty double meanings, and this carries over into the Greek as well, and one such example is relevant to the mythic hymn we find in Philippians - with which we began this section.

In my undergraduate degree I took six semesters of *Koine* Greek and two of biblical Hebrew. I wish I retained more of that knowledge than I do but what I do remember, vividly, was my senior year during which I attended Synagogue.

During my last two semesters both my Hebrew and my Greek professors asked us to attend the only local Jewish temple in town. It was a small community of about two dozen or so elderly worshipers, so small in fact that they did not have their own Rabbi. They had to ask one to drive the 3 hours down from Dallas one Friday a month. We were grateful for their allowing us to worship with them, and during this period two interesting points of learning converged from my two classes. From our Hebrew readings, my professor had always requested that we take the divine name "*Yahweh*" and replace it with the title "*Adonai*," meaning Lord. This, she explained, was the way that the Jewish people read the text so as to avoid pronouncing the name of God. Her instruction was wisely given, as the synagogue community graciously welcomed us and were so hospitable as to ask us on a few occasions to read the Torah portion during temple. When reading a passage that contained God's name, we substituted, "*Adonai*," the Lord.

For my first two years of Greek we had spent our time in the gospels and epistles, where we had often discussed the wordplay of the early church in using the Greek word *Kyrios* (Lord) for Jesus as a direct challenge to the Roman Empire. In a world such as the first century levant - where it is decreed that Caesar is Lord, the son of a god, and King unto the ends of the Earth - it begins to make sense how the claim that Jesus is Lord, son of God, and has a message about the coming Kingdom of Heaven becomes a direct challenge to the powers that be. It is no accident that those who encounter Jesus assume the Messiah is going to restore the Kingdom of Israel and drive out the foreign occupiers. Nor is it a coincidence that Jesus is killed in a manner that was saved for political radicals. Those hung on a cross were traitors to the Empire, their means of execution a display of the might of Rome to all who would challenge their Lord, Caesar.

So in the context of the New Testament authors we have "Lord" used in place of the divine name in Jewish scripture (which is inherently political in a theocratic culture), and as a political (while also religious, as a part of the imperial cult) title in the wider Roman culture. And it is in the Septuagint - the Greek translation of the Hebrew Bible - that these converge. The translation of the Hebrew *Adonai* into Greek is, again, *Kyrios*. All of this, I realize, can seem a bit academic, but I hope you are beginning to see how the stage is set. How is it, we might ask, that Jesus of Nazareth can be killed as a blasphemer by the Jewish people and a political dissident by Rome when he is only wandering the countryside preaching a message of forgiveness of Sin and repentance? And we find our answer in Paul's hymn:

> *"[Christ Jesus] emptied himself, taking the form of a slave, born in human likeness. And being found in human form, he humbled himself and became obedient to the point of death, even death on a cross. Therefore God exalted him to the highest place, and gave him the name that is above every name, so that at the name of Jesus every knee should bend, in heaven and on earth and under the earth, and every tongue should confess that Jesus Christ is Lord"* - Phil. 2:7-11

Jesus, the Messiah, is *Kyrios*. This is the church's confession about the risen Christ, but it is the identity which gets him killed in the first place. By his very identity, Rome is challenged, because Caesar is not *Lord*. Jesus is. And by his very identity, the authority of the Temple is challenged, because where does the Spirit of the *Lord* dwell? In Jesus. And who speaks for the *Lord*? As the scribes ask, "Why does this fellow speak in this way? It is blasphemy! Who can forgive sins but God alone?" (Mark 2:7). But the Lord speaks for the Lord's own self.

This is the irony and paradox at the heart of the cross: that in being executed for challenging the notions of who is *Lord*, the Christ fulfills the very task which makes him worthy of the name - refusal to grasp for equality with God, but humble obedience to the point of death. It is here that we begin to see how Jesus is "like God." For God has given the Christ God's own name. But he has received this name for trusting that he does not need to overreach his form as a human being and try to "be like God." This is a human being who accepts what it means to be a human being. One who does not consider equality with God something to be grasped for. Given the same temptation that the rest of us have been failing to overcome since Genesis, Jesus chooses not to overreach but to empty himself in humility. How could such a one as this not become intolerable to the order of things? By his very existence he reveals the lies that we tell about ourselves, about our world, and about the nature of God. We cannot be free to continue our pursuit to "be like God" without answering the challenge of this one who already is. When Jesus - in obedience to his nature - refuses to yield to our expectations of a messiah, we reject him. And when his identity cannot be co-opted, and the systems and powers that we have created to cover over ourselves cannot pervert or discredit him, what option is there left except either to accept or to destroy him?

As we have seen, Jesus uses the creative capacity that we all possess as a namer and shaper of reality. And he uses it to deconstruct the institutions that we have built to cover our nakedness and control our world as if we are like God. In this way, Jesus takes on institutionalized Sin and reveals the true Kingdom. And the Christ uses the same capacity we have for relationship - as a mirror he displayed a fulfilled vision of human identity: a vision which calls out how often we use others and allow ourselves to be used in a desire to find meaning, identity, and belonging. In this way Jesus models the deep vulnerability and rootedness in God that is required for Sinlessness. Jesus modeled that when one places their trust so deeply in this God that they are willing to empty themselves and accept their own death and nakedness, the power of these things to destroy is revealed in its own limitedness. Death is not the final arbiter. And those who imitate Christ need not fear it, because shame and death have *power* in this world, but they do not have *authority* over God's anointed.

This begins to answer the question, "What is Jesus like?" He is like us, and he is like God. But is the inverse true? Jesus being like us does not necessarily mean that we are like him. That comes as we grow in discipleship. And Jesus is like God, but to what extent can we truly claim that God is like the Christ? We must turn now to this larger and more mysterious question.

Section IV

What Is God Like?

Chapter 11

God's Place in the Order of Things

Moses was keeping the flock of his father-in-law Jethro, the priest of Midian; he led his flock beyond the wilderness, and came to Horeb, the mountain of God. There the angel of the Lord appeared to him in a flame of fire out of a bush; he looked, and the bush was blazing, yet it was not consumed. Then Moses said, "I must turn aside and look at this great sight, and see why the bush is not burned up." When the Lord saw that he had turned aside to see, God called to him out of the bush, "Moses, Moses!" And he said, "Here I am." The God said, "Come no closer! Remove the sandals from your feet, for the place on which you are standing is holy ground." God said further, "I am the God of your father, the God of Abraham, the God of Isaac, and the God of Jacob." And Moses hid his face, for he was afraid to look at God.

Then the Lord said, "I have observed the misery of my people who are in Egypt; I have heard their cry on account of their taskmasters. Indeed, I know their sufferings, and I have come down to deliver them from the Egyptians, and to bring them up out of that land to a good and broad land, a land flowing with milk and honey...So come, I will send you to Pharaoh to bring my people, the Israelites out of Egypt." But Moses said to God, "Who

am I that I should go to Pharaoh, and bring the Israelites out of
Egypt?" God said, "I will be with you; and this shall be the sign for
you that it is I who sent you: when you have brought the people out
of Egypt, you shall worship God on this mountain."

But Moses said to God, "If I come to the Israelites and say to them,
'The God of your ancestors has sent me to you,' and they ask me,
'What is his name?' what shall I say to them?" God said to Moses, "I
AM WHO I AM." God said further, "Thus you shall say to the
Israelites, 'I AM has sent me to you.'
-Exodus 3:1-14[24]

In the last section we discussed my experience in synagogue of
substituting the divine name. God's name, in Judaism, is considered too
holy to say, so instead one typically calls God, "the Lord." But one
convenience we did not mention is that this avoids the paradox of trying to
keep hold of God's name. "Lord" is a title I can understand and by which I
can measure the identity of God. But we find in the story above that God's
true name is much wilier. In the ancient world, knowing the name of a deity
meant that an individual had some power over it, they could invoke a spirit
or a god in order to solicit their aid. But who did this God say to call upon? "I
am." So who is this God? God is. What does God's name teach us to expect of
God? That God will be who God will be. And in this passage, we leave with
an insight into what it is like to be in relationship with this God: God *is. Is*
the God of Abraham, Isaac, and Jacob. *Is* aware of the suffering of God's
people. *Is* working in the world to God's own ends. *Is* refusing to be anything
other than who God wishes to be.

---

[24] Alter renders this as "I will be who I will be," arguing that the logic of the divine
name "would be that whereas particular actions may be attributed to humans through the
verbal names chosen for them, to God alone belongs unlimited, unconditional being." See Alter,
The Five Books of Moses, 321-322.

So, who does God wish to be? This is a more difficult question. As we previously discussed, God's own anointed one was killed for blasphemy. This should stand to remind us how easy it is to confuse our theologies with the being and identity of God. But I want to take seriously here the power of names. What can we draw from this scripture - and from the unfolding of the covenant relationship which emerges from it - to help us understand what God is *like*? I would, again, like to limit our observations to three things from the passage in question. First, God is holy. When Moses approaches, he cannot look directly at God. He removes his sandals as an acknowledgment of the transcendent presence into which he is entering. Second, God has a people. When God wishes to reveal something about God's own identity, it is the relationships in which God has engaged which are recalled: Abraham, Isaac, Jacob, "the cries of *my* people in Egypt." And finally, that God is self-defined. In a world in which we cannot help but talk about God, and in which theology must be responsible for the claim that God is and the judgement that God is God, ultimately the being and identity of God answer for themselves, when they answer.

Chapter 12

Mysterium Tremendum

I inherited from my father an intense - and, to some people, unsettling - fascination with fire. As a child I would sit in front of our fireplace at home, or the campfire when out in the woods and watch the flickering and dancing of the flames. Often, I would secretly feed various small things into the fire while trying to avoid both burning my fingers and the reprimands of my mother. Something about the constrained power of a "controlled burn" and the inability of my mind to categorize the nature of fire - it being in no recognizable state of matter - never fails to captivate my attention with a mix of curiosity and fearful respect. It seems fitting, then, that in our passage, here, the presence of God manifests itself as a wildfire. The spectacle draws Moses to it, but he can only approach so far before he realizes that the untamed otherness of this experience demands respect. Unshod, he proceeds, unsure of what to expect, as he is standing on holy ground.

Again, I marvel at the imagination of Scripture to so aptly point toward a difficult theological reality: i.e. holiness. In my own upbringing, and in much of the popular theology I have come across, to "be holy" seemed to indicate a degree of ethical character. Holiness as complete goodness, a culmination of every perfect moral aspect. But we find a different picture in the epiphany at the burning bush. Before Moses knows almost anything about the character of this being, prior to knowing the name or actions or identity of this one, its power and otherness are evident. The recognition of God's holiness precedes a sense of precisely whose presence it is we have entered. This is a point worth our consideration in thinking about what God is like and how to speak about and be in relationship with this God in our own context.

The Fear of the Lord

There is a certain Marcionism,[25] I think, across most American Christianity. Both in churches and among the Lost there seems to be a general sense that the God of the Old Testament is not the same God as in the New. Perhaps, some friends tell me, it is simply a personality change or - as I've heard others speculate - they are two distinct beings: that the God whom Jesus calls "Father" is not the same as the God of Israel. Such speculations run deep in a post-Christendom context and must be dealt with if we seek to keep Scripture at the center of our disciple-making work.

Reflecting on my own encounters with this struggle over orthodoxy, I think a lot of this disharmony comes from trying to maintain the tension between love and fear. Most people I meet, regardless of their level of biblical education, have been told that Christians believe God is love - or at least is loving. And this seems incompatible with the recurring fear we encounter in the stories throughout the Hebrew Bible. As most of our churches in NYC start by studying in the gospels, this conversation almost inevitably comes up the first time we turn to the Old Testament and encounter passages where this fear is present and even encouraged; when we are told things like "the fear of the Lord is the beginning of wisdom" (Proverbs 9:10). If perfect love drives out fear, and God is love, then how and why would we fear God? This is one of the early and most ubiquitous questions in our disciple-making work.

---

[25] Marcion of Sinope was a second century teacher who believed in Jesus as a savior sent from God but rejected the Hebrew God as an evil and inferior spiritual being from whom humanity had to be saved by the God of the New Testament. For more see, Justo L. Gonzalez, *The Story of Christianity* (Prince Press: New York, NY, 2010), 61-62.

In the initial years of being in church with Mary and Rebekah I recall this issue coming up frequently. As they had friends and family members die, as my and Rebekah's marriages fell apart, as they went through job losses and encountered unresolved relational strife in their first seasons of faith, the recurring refrain was: "God is punishing us." And this is a common view among my friends and neighbors in a post-Christendom context: that God's desire is to condemn and to punish, this is why we should be afraid. Because we have offended God's holiness, we must constantly anticipate that punitive consequences are around the corner. I have been told many times - including by people who are not, themselves, theists - that the nature of the God of Scripture requires that God destroy or drive out anything that would tarnish God's sanctity. Even among my friends who are not inclined to believe in a personal God, there exists a sort of deistic karma: a framework in which bad actions result in punishing consequences and opportunity is the result of virtuous living.

It seems to me that this picture of God is effective if our desire is to keep people conscious of their moral failings and the many ways in which we perpetuate Sin and brokenness in the world. But does it point us toward the deeper reality of what the character and identity of God are *actually* like? Is the type of fear we produce in those we spiritually form conducive to better revealing the Truth toward which theology seeks to gesture? These are questions I am not equipped to answer with any certainty. In our work, the most honest way I know how to respond is - again - through the sharing of my own experiences of God in worship.

No other gods before God

I spoke in a previous chapter about my prayer practice. My own spirituality is deeply informed by the contemplative tradition and I identify as a mystic. Confessionally, I find that difficult to admit in many Christian circles. Mysticism was not a category with which I was raised, and it still conjures up for me images of new age or spiritualist gurus: I fear having and being perceived as having a deluded sense of my own spiritual perceptions and experiences. On the other hand, I do seek to cultivate a contemplative disposition in those that I disciple. This, as mentioned in the previous section, is in an attempt to reflect the deep rootedness in God that we see as a facet of Jesus. And the first principle in which I coach my friends and house church leaders on in prayer is what I refer to as "aimlessness."

When we enter into silent prayer, I tell them, we go with no agenda and no expectations. Contemplation is not a means to an end, but an end unto itself. We do not go into prayer seeking to accomplish anything, but simply to be attentive to God and to be sufficiently present to encounter whatever, if anything, it is God wishes to reveal or speak. There are many emotions that accompany this practice: anxiety, insecurity, boredom, frustration, etc. But one of the early revelations in silent prayer, and one of the primary reasons it is so tempting to avoid entering into this space, is a feeling of surrendering control. When we stop talking, when we quiet the mental chatter, we find ourselves deeply vulnerable and at the mercy of another's will.

Because if God gets to do whatever God likes in prayer, then I do not - unless my desires are aligned with God's. And what if God fails to attend to my wants and needs? What if God chooses to do nothing? What if God chooses to reveal things that I wish to avoid or thought were already resolved? Or chooses to ask something of me which I am not prepared to give? Beneath the other emotions and reactions to joining God in silent contemplation, especially in the beginning, there is almost always a deep fear. Even in the experience of God's love, as we saw earlier, I am only able to participate in the love and acceptance of the divine as the person that I truly am.

Put another way, because God loves us, God seeks to dispel the broken unrealities in which we live. And the "self" that I imagine and project to others is too often one of these idols. So God's loving presence comes at the cost of participating in God's reality: one in which I am a person of unclean lips and belong to a people of unclean lips (Isaiah 6:5); and one in which I surrender control over who I wish God to be and allow God to be who God wishes. So it is not necessarily punishment I fear, but the reality of God. The very being and identity of God induces fear in me, because it brings with it - however momentarily - the power to unmask idols and reveal Truth. And in the words of David Foster Wallace, "The truth will set you free. But not until it's finished with you."[26]

This experience of God is what Rudolf Otto refers to as the *mysterium tremendum*.[27] It is the manifestation of mystery and awe that attracts us toward a numinous embrace and causes us to hide our faces in dread of its overwhelming majesty. The holiness of God burns like a fire that does not consume. In a context where we worship God however we wish to conceive of God, few things should induce more fear than encountering the God who is: because the experience of God comes at the cost of experiencing Reality. For those who would wish to speak truly about the God of scripture in the world, it is high time we learn again how to speak about what this "holy one" is *like*.

---

[26] David Foster Wallace, *Infinite Jest* (Back Bay Books: New York, NY, 1996), 389.
[27] Rudolf Otto, *The Idea of the Holy* (Oxford University Press: London, 1923), 12-15.

Chapter 13

God and God's People

I was raised in a denomination known as the Churches of Christ, which are a part of the Stone-Campbell/Restoration Movement. The foundational intentions behind my particular tradition were to overcome the creedal and institutional divisions of Protestantism by returning to *Sola Scriptura* and restoring the New Testament church. Confessionally, my experience has been that the result of our efforts was less the church of Acts and more a network of congregations frequently in conflict with one another and with denominations around us over who embodied the "true faith" of Christ's church.

With no larger institution to bind us beyond personal interpretations of Scripture, in order to retain our own distinct religious identity, we frequently disfellowshipped or cut ourselves off from anyone who diverged from our own understandings of the Bible. And by isolating ourselves from the larger memory of how Christian faith has operated throughout history and in various contexts, my fellowship has often been ill equipped to imagine any faithful way of living in the world beyond our own experience. My denomination encapsulates, I think, one of the more interesting features of Protestant religion which I get to see manifested in its post-Christendom expression: its ahistoricism.

Most of us don't spend a great deal of time thinking about where we come from and the historical forces that shape our identities and affiliations.

We like to pretend that there is a direct line between "our founding fathers" (whomever that may be contextually) and our particular practices and beliefs, with no people or processes of change in between. This is a feature of our political culture as Americans as much as it is our religious culture, and it has been inherited as a part of the spirituality of the Lost. The ability to identify with and embrace spiritualities apart from "religion"[28] is predicated on adopting those practices and identities without necessitating a sense of commonality or institutional ties to the historical communities which existed between their origin and our own time, and which developed and preserved them.

So, one may be Christian in their "personal faith" and reject church and/or traditional theology, venerate Buddha and disregard the idea of Mara or the Dharma, convert to Islam but not observe Halal or go to Masjid, etc. And this reality is distinct from being nominally religious: that is, affiliated with a faith in name alone, but without any serious observance. For many in our context, the choosing and blending of religious identities *does* bring about a sense of meaning and spiritual renewal in their lives, and they see their spirituality as a central part of themselves. Simply one that is not subject to those bodies which preceded them in or share that same identity. For the Lost, most feel that they are entitled to determine for themselves what it means to be "x," and should not have to yield to the ways in which that identity has been previously defined or embodied.

This is a reality which our team struggles to navigate in our church planting work in NYC. How do we plant communities of faith among the Lost who are free to interpret and redefine aspects of faith, but do not see themselves as the sole restoration or embodiment of God's work in the world? How do we try to leave behind some of the dysfunctional and misguided incarnations of Christian faith, while remaining in solidarity with

---

[28] And of the more than a quarter of Americans who identify as religiously unaffiliated, (or "nones") one of the most frequent self-designations (>37%) is "Spiritual-But-Not-Religious." Elizabeth Drescher, *Choosing Our Religion* (Oxford University Press: New York, NY, 2016), 16-22.

the church of God that already exists? Once again, I have no easy answers, but I think it is worth discussing why this is an important value in our context.

Believing vs Belonging

I realize that, in what I have just said, it would be easy to conclude that individualism is at the heart of faith for the Lost. In many senses this is correct. It is my professional opinion, however, that most people seek out and long for spiritual community. As we discussed previously, human beings have an innate sense that "it is not good to be alone," and - even in a privatized and individualistic religious culture - we often seek out mirroring relationships. The inability to share and learn from the faith of others is one of the most presenting hurts I find in many of my friends and neighbors. For this reason, evangelism is not actually that difficult to initiate as many people want to speak about spiritual things, they simply fear being coerced or disrespected by others in conversations around faith. The Lost frequently seek out meaningful spiritual community, but all too consistently find that the foundations upon which they try to establish belonging prove artificial.

In my early training in missions, there was a popular paradigm which was often discussed which we called "Belong, Believe, Become." The function of this framework was to play with the sequence of these three experiences and see how they shaped ministry among a particular group of people. For example, in many traditional models of evangelism, one first *believes* the tenets of Christian faith, so *becomes* a Christian (generally through baptism or saying the sinner's prayer), this brings a status of *belonging* in the church. In other models, one may first find *belonging* among a community of people, so begin to adopt the *beliefs* of that group, thus *becoming* one of them. The intersection of these experiences is something I continue to reflect on with respect to the desire for belonging which exists among the Lost as they simultaneously seek to be self-determining in their beliefs: what does it mean to belong to a group of people if you do not share their beliefs and practices? Is it possible to share beliefs and identification with a people but not belong among them in any meaningful way?

One of the best illustrations of this same issue comes in the form of the fictional religion of Bokononism in Kurt Vonnegut's classic sci-fi novel, *Cat's Cradle*. In Vonnegut's tale, the main character converts from Christianity to a Caribbean cult created by a disenchanted WWI veteran. Vonnegut's story makes frequent breaks from the primary narrative to explain facets of this fictitious system of belief, and in regard to spiritual community the narrator says the following:

> *We Bokononists believe that humanity is organized into teams, teams that do God's Will without ever discovering what they are doing. Such a team is called a karass...'If you find your life tangles up with somebody else's life for no very logical reasons,' writes Bokonon, 'that person may be a member of your karass.'*[29]

In a later scene, the narrator is on a cross-country flight and discovers that his seatmate is a native of Indiana (a "Hoosier"), which is also where he hails from. He is quickly annoyed at her attempt to bond with him over such a superficial fact, stating

> *Hazel's obsession with Hoosiers around the world was a textbook example of a false karass, of a seeming team that was meaningless in terms of the ways God gets things done, a textbook example of what Bokonon calls a granfalloon. Other examples of granfalloons are the Communist party, the Daughters of the American Revolution, the General Electric Company, the International Order of Odd Fellows -- and any nation, anytime, anywhere.*[30]

---

[29] Kurt Vonnegut, *Cats Cradle* (Dial Trade Paperbacks: New York, NY, 2010), 1-2.
[30] *Ibid.* 91-92.

If we may borrow Vonnegut's language, we might pose the question in this way: as the Lost seek out spiritual belonging, and as those of us in ministry in a post-Christendom context seek to create communities of spiritual belonging among the Lost, how do we know whether we are establishing a *karass* or a *granfalloon*? While this may at first seem like a solely ecclesiological question,[31] I would like to turn now to attend to how this sense of belonging is actually rooted in the identity of the God we find in our text in Exodus. Because, as I hope we shall see, belonging among a people is an important feature of understanding what God is *like*.

The God of your Father

'I am the God of your father, the God of Abraham, the God of Isaac, and the God of Jacob.' And Moses hid his face, for he was afraid to look at God.Then the Lord said, 'I have observed the misery of my people who are in Egypt; I have heard their cry on account of their taskmasters. Indeed, I know their sufferings, and I have come down to deliver them from the Egyptians, and to bring them up out of that land to a good and broad land, a land flowing with milk and honey...So come, I will send you to Pharaoh to bring my people, the Israelites out of Egypt'
-Exodus 3:6-10

In the previous chapter we discussed the way in which the holiness of God has the power to strip away the idols and unrealities which we create. I would suggest to you that there are few idols as subtle and pernicious as our historical memories. The power to shape memory is the power to shape the future. It is the authority upon which we establish so many of the games we play - such potent principalities and powers as race, political sovereignty, national identity, etc. And it is why the passage in question is so provocative

---

[31] Ecclesiology being the theological study of "church."

and subversive in our context: because the God of Scripture is one who has entered into history and chosen to be known through particular relationships. And in pursuing the identity of God, we find our lives entangled with the lives of others who we would otherwise have no logical reason with which to engage.

Because, if I am taking it on Jesus' authority, the God whose anointed one he is is the God depicted in the Hebrew Bible. Which means that the God that I encounter in prayer is the same one who rescued Israel out of slavery. And the God who allowed God's own covenant people to be taken into exile is the same one to whom I desire to be reconciled. The experiences of violence and judgement I find in Scripture must be dealt with as facets of the same being which I believe to be the very epitome of mercy and love. And the churches I seek to plant read the same Scriptures and draw from the same bank of theological language as those churches which helped colonize the "new world" and have supported various political kingdoms both past and present.

Because God has chosen to participate in history, part of coming to an awareness of what God is *like* necessitates that I take seriously the history of those who have been in relationship with God. And this is not to suggest that every account of God is of equal revelatory value. Or that every interpretation of God's actions by God's people is an accurate reflection of God's character and intention.[32] Or even that God cannot choose to be other than how God has acted or been understood to act in the past. Simply that a large part of choosing to be in a relationship with this God involves inheriting God's history of relationships, for good or ill. It involves being adopted into a lineage of people with diverse experiences and convictions about what this being is *like* and having to deal with these assertions as we work out the truth of the claims of those who preceded us in faith.

And this brings with it the obligation to enter into an ongoing conversation with the people of God - our *karass* - and to test and evaluate

---

[32] As Scharlemann reminded us, theology is often wrong in its assertions.

the spectrum of experiences that we find there. God's participating in history means that the identity and being of God must be dealt with outside of my immediate experience of God, and that of my surrounding community. Because the God whom Jesus invites us to follow has chosen to be known through not only our lives but those which preceded us. Thus, in our context, we must take seriously that when we encounter this holy one and would ask, "Who are you?," one of the primary answers is the God of Abraham, Isaac, and Jacob.

To belong to this one is to accept that we are grafted into a team which has been working as agents of reconciliation - though often erringly - from before we arrived on the scene. History is a facet of the identity of God. So, if we find ourselves outside of relationship with those God has identified with before us, it seems we must ask: is this the God of Jesus whom we are seeking, or someone else? Are we part of God's people or have we joined a *granfalloon*?

Chapter 14

The Divine Name

Working in New York City has enabled me to pursue a pet project that was less available to me in previous years and places where I worked: studying the architecture of Christian worship. I live within an easy commute of Saint Patrick's Cathedral, which is as ornate as any church I've seen in Europe; my neighborhood is littered with storefront Pentecostal churches of various cultural backgrounds, there is a large Greek Orthodox congregation not far from my favorite sushi spot, and Manhattan hosts many thriving non-denominational places of worship which have greatly influenced the church planting world in North America and around the globe. This diverse sampling of how churches can be designed and function affords an interesting case study in worship, not purely through a programmatic lens but also in regard to the literal space that they occupy. Because how we arrange the context in which we worship says a lot about what is important to us in worship.

For example, in the congregations in which I was raised, you will find a consistent layout: a main aisle leads to a pulpit at the center of a stage which will almost always stand in front of or right next to a baptistry. This is no coincidence as preaching, teaching, and baptism are of central importance in my heritage's theology, and this is reflected in our worship space. Catholic churches, by contrast, have the altar upon which the Eucharist is celebrated front and center. The lectern is usually to the side as the purpose and central function of Mass is the dispensation of the transubstantiated body and blood in taking communion. Unlike the "auditorium" of the churches in which I was raised, worship there takes place in the "sanctuary," and this difference in language reflects a difference in theology regarding the purpose and function of the worship space.

And this rule is true beyond Christianity. Most of the mosques around me are simple and unadorned apartments or storefronts, designed to allow convenient spaces for believers to come and pray five times a day. The Hindu temples I've visited in Queens contain the many images of the gods worshiped there as well as space for the food and festivals which accompany their religious practice. And in the ancient world, too, we gain insight into worship through its spatial arrangement: because at the center of an ancient temple is the image of the god worshiped there. As one proceeds into the holiest space - at the center of importance of the temple of Baal, of Dagon, of Mithras, of Artemis, etc - there one will find the representation of the deity. Which highlights the contrast of Israel's temple. Because at the center of Israel's Holy of Holies sits the ark of the covenant, topped with cherubim whose wings form the mercy seat.[33] The most sacred space where the image of God would sit holds, instead, an empty throne. Because for those that worship the one whose very name is *Being*, no idol can sit in the place of God. No image can occupy the throne of God, and faithful worship, then, puts nothing in the place where only God belongs.

Which brings us back to our passage in question: "What is your name?' What shall I say to them? asks Moses of God in the burning bush. And God says, "Tell them, I am who I am," or "I will be who I will be." Because God is self-defined. No other name, no other image, nothing else will answer for God except God's own self. But how do we worship one such

---

[33] Alter describes the cherubim in Exodus 25:17-22 as "fearsome winged beasts (compare the Egyptian sphinx) that figure in poetry as God's celestial steeds and that here serve as His terrestrial throne, 'enthroned upon cherubim' being an epithet for the deity." Alter, *The Five Books of Moses*, 462. See also Alter's note on cherubim on the Ark as "the earthly 'throne' of the invisible deity." Robert Alter, *The David Story: A Translation with Commentary of 1 and 2 Samuel* (W. W. Norton and Company: New York, NY, 1999), 22.

as this? And who is it that God chooses to be? Almost any notion or image we can point to begins to break down. Is God a judge? When God chooses to be. Is God a father? A king? A whirlwind? A hen gathering her chicks under the shelter of her wings? These images may point to God, to help us understand the nature and identity of God. But, like all theology, they do not speak for God. They fail in their ability to define. God will be who God will be, and God speaks for God's own self. That is God's nature and name. But we have here the paradox of the incarnation. For there is another who claims to speak for God. One who claims oneness with God. There is another in Scripture who when asked to identify himself answers, "I am" (John 6:20; 8:24-28; 18:4-8). Jesus of Nazareth makes these claims. The God who throughout history has - despite carrying many titles - refused to be confined by any other *name* or image is the one whom Jesus claims to embody and speak for. For those of us that wish to follow him as disciples, we must then ask: How Christlike is our God?

The Biblical Canon

As might be expected from the pluralism of our context, one of the frequent questions which emerges at the beginning of our churches forming is why we are reading the Bible. At times this is presented as a challenge, "What could we possibly learn from a book as old and as problematic as the Bible?" that people seem to be suggesting (and sometimes literally asking). "Why just the Bible and not every religious text?" others inquire. And my answer to this array of questions is fairly consistent. I tell those forming these new groups that anything they read and find spiritually stimulating I think they should be welcome to bring into our conversations, but the reason I think Scripture should be at the center of our conversation is because the Bible is already carrying on a similar conversation when we enter into it. Across the library that makes up the Old and New Testaments, we encounter a dialogue spanning the breadth of history about who this God is and what it means for us as human beings. There is ample disharmony among the authors of Scripture, and this is in part because of the diversity of contexts and experiences from which they write. But throughout the Bible, they are engaged in a conversation - working to challenge one another and collaboratively piece together a grand story through poetry and genealogy, through history and myth - surrounding this same being and identity of God in human history and the implications thereof. And this is the same conversation our churches are carrying on.

So, if someone in our churches wants to bring their own reading and study and experiences into conversation with Scripture, I want them to. But, I say, let's measure those things within the conversation already taking place in Scripture. And I choose the word *measure* intentionally, because that is the nature of canon. When we use that language about the Bible, that it is "canonical" or these books are "the canon," we are borrowing that language from the Greek word which means "standard" or "rule" (as in a ruler to measure).[34] Canon is the measure of the experience of the people of God. It is the standard by which we evaluate our own experiences and practices. By entering into the conversation taking place there we are challenged to reckon with those of other times and contexts and to compare their theologies to our own. This is how I explain the centrality of Scripture to my friends. And Jesus, I explain, is the canon within the canon. In the same way that I want us to measure our experiences and dialogue about God by the conversation taking place in Scripture, I want us to measure the picture of God depicted in Scripture by the person of Jesus. As the many authors and communities which have formed the canon make claims and describe experiences of God, let us measure those by the canon of the Christ.

The Canon of Christ

So, in what way is Christ the measure of Scripture? And in what sense does this make Jesus the measure of God? This is the crux of the

---

[34] See Frederick William Danker, *The Concise Greek-English Lexicon of the New Testament* (University of Chicago Press: Chicago, IL. 2009), 187.

Christian faith: that at the intersection of Scripture and our own context is not a set of theological propositions, is not a creed, is not simply a book. There is a person. That when the Word of God wished to be defined and to dwell among us it took on not pages but flesh. And if theology is "talking about God" then to talk about Jesus is, by definition, theology.

When we wish to see the picture of what a human being is *like* when restored to our rightful image, we find Jesus of Nazareth. The image of the invisible God which was placed in Eden finds its restoration and its embodiment in the prophet from Galilee. And the anointed one, the Messiah who the Scriptures anticipate, as he washes the feet of his disciples, says they are right to call him "Lord" and "Master" (John 13). Which is to say that - to use Scharlemann's definition - if the being and identity of God answer for themselves; Jesus claims that, in him, they have answered. So how Christlike is God? As much as God has chosen to be. It is not through Aristolilean logic or meditation on first principles of philosophy that we come to this conclusion, but through a conviction about the nature of God. God will be who God will be. And God has chosen to be Jesus, the Christ. So when we encounter this same Holy One, the God of Abraham, Isaac, and Jacob, who is on mission to redeem the world and reconcile all things, and when we are called in our context as coworkers in this reconciliation we might find ourselves - like Moses - asking, "When they ask me, what is the name of this God? What shall I tell them?" And the answer God has chosen - the only one to whom God has given God's own name - is Jesus.

Conclusion

Not long ago (as of this writing) KJ and I were on a silent retreat in upstate New York. It has been my annual practice for going on a decade to get away for a week or so to be in solitude and try to reorient myself in faith and ministry, and for the last couple of years it has worked out in KJ's schedule for her to join me. This particular trip we were accompanied by another friend of ours, a devout Buddhist who participates with our gathering in the East Village, and on one of the days we were briefly breaking silence for an evening walk. "Have you seen the river?" my friend asked me. "Is that a movie?" I replied. "No, the Genesee River that runs by here." he answered. "Oh!" I responded, "No. But I saw it on the map." The next day I went walking deep into the woods and when I came back to the monastery I was drenched in sweat and more than a little sunburnt. When I spoke with KJ about it later she asked if I had found the river. "No, I replied, but I did get in trouble with a monk for being on a private road." When she asked where I was at the time, I described the place to her and she gently replied, "The river is actually on the opposite end of that road. It's in the other direction when you're leaving the monastery."

I tell this story because it is akin to the process of composing this book. As I stated at the beginning, I have tried to speak truly about God and in many ways likely failed to do so. The being and identity of God answer for themselves, when they answer. Even so, it has often been the case that I have poured over this or that section of writing only to go over it with my friends and be told, "Actually what you're looking for is in the opposite direction. You're going the wrong way." For this, and for allowing me to share parts of their stories, I deeply thank them (you all know who you are).

We began this work with an ethnography of Lostness, and an acknowledgement that our context calls for a theological reorientation, to help us speak more truly about God (the central task of theology) so that Truth might be seen and heard. It is my hope that the experiences of our churches made up of Lost people and my efforts to tell our stories have left you better equipped to enter into relationship with the Lost and speak more truly of God. I hope you arrive at this point more able to acknowledge the continuing degree of your own Lostness, so that we might all together continue to seek after God.

It has also been my experience in writing this that I have frequently found myself stuck in a section. During those times I have generally either slammed my laptop shut, often adding a quick, "This is why Jesus didn't write any books!" under my breath, or I have slipped into fantasizing about how this will end up being received. I confess that too often the desire to complete this work has been an attempt for me to fill up "the void," a means of seeking affirmation and acceptance. Too frequently it has been a way for me to present a better version of myself that does not correspond as closely as it should to the person that I am (even writing those last few sentences, I have to question whether this, too, is a bid to *seem* authentic). It is my hope that my friends and editors have helped me to remedy that as much as possible, but I raise the point to confess again that this book embodies exactly what we have discussed about what it is like to be human: it has been my desire to be creative and reshape some things, it is the product of much time spent in solitude and has been refined through the mirroring of my community, and it contains within it my own weaknesses and limitations.

This is what it is like to be human. But we see in the person of Jesus a means of working out our humanity in such a way as to escape the temptation to overreach and "to be like God" (Gen. 3:5), thus becoming what we were created to be. In some strange and paradoxical way, this is the revelation of God: the holy and self-defining one who has, inexplicably, chosen to enter into history and become known through a relationship with humanity. And in our acceptance that we are not created to be "like God," we allow God to be who God will be (Ex. 3:14), and we discover in this one's anointed, Jesus - "who, though being in the very nature of God, did not consider equality with God something to be grasped for" (Phil. 2:6) - what

God is truly like. This is the profound theological tension that Jesus, the Christ, lives within - the tightrope walk of Christian theology - and (I believe) how it is that the being and identity of God have chosen to answer for themselves.

Bibliography

Alter, R. (1999). *The David Story: A Translation with Commentary of 1 and 2 Samuel*. New York: W. W. Norton and Company.

Alter, R. (2004). *The Five Books of Moses: A Translation with Commentary*. New York: W.W. Norton & Company.

Danker, F.W. (2009). *The Concise Greek-English Lexicon of the New Testament*. Chicago: University of Chicago Press.

Drescher, E. (2016). *Choosing Our Religion*. New York: Oxford University Press.

Friedman, M. (1991). The Island of Stone Money. *Working Papers in Economics, 91*(3), 1-3.

Gonzalez, J.L. (2010). *The Story of Christianity*. New York: Prince Press.

Grenz, S.J. (1994). *Theology for the Community of God*. Grand Rapids: Eerdmans.

Looney, J. (2015). *Crossroads of the Nations*. Portland: Urban Loft Publishers.

Looney, J., & Bouchelle, S. (2017). *Mosaic: A Ministry Handbook for a Globalizing World*. Skyforest, CA: Urban Loft Publishers.

Murray, S. (2004). *Post-Christendom: Church and Ministry in a Strange New World*. Colorado Springs, CO: Paternoster Press.

Otto, R. (1923). *The Idea of the Holy*. London: Oxford University Press.

Scharlemann, R.P. (1981). *The Being of God: Theology and the Experience of Truth*. New York: Seabury Press.

de la Torre, M.A. (2004). *Santeria: The Beliefs and Rituals of a Growing Religion in America*. Grand Rapids: Eerdmans.

Vonnegut, K. (2010). *Cat's Cradle*. New York: Dial Trade Paperbacks.

Wallace, D.F. (1996). *Infinite Jest*. New York: Back Bay Books.

Ward, B. (2003). *The Desert Fathers: Sayings of the Early Christian Monks*. London: Penguin Press.

Wink, W. (2003). *Jesus and Nonviolence: A Third Way*. Minneapolis, MN: Fortress Press.